Wildflowers

A School Superintendent's Challenge to America

by Jonathan P. Raymond

Cover Art & Design by Peter H. Reynolds, FableVision

Published in the United States by SF Press, an imprint of the
Stuart Foundation, San Francisco.
www.stuartfoundation.org

ISBN 978-1-7321416-0-5
Subject Codes: EDU001040; EDU032000; EDU34000

Printed in the United States of America

Book design by FableVision Studios
Jacket design by Peter H. Reynolds
Additional Contributions by Paul A. Reynolds

First Edition

"At a time when our nation is looking for a new, more humane and inspiring vision to guide education into the 21st century, Jonathan Raymond has provided the background and framework for constructing and implementing such a vision in our nation's most challenged and disadvantaged schools. Drawing on his experience as an educational leader in Boston, Charlotte, and Sacramento, Raymond explains why a holistic vision that makes it possible to address the needs of the 'whole' child—intellectual, emotional, social, and physical—is so essential. In writing that is clear and compelling, Raymond shows us how this can be done and why it is so necessary.

"For anyone looking for insights and ideas, and who understands why education is so critical to democracy and to our future as a society, this book will serve as a practical guide and a source of inspiration."

—Pedro A. Noguera, PhD, UCLA Graduate School of Education & Information Studies

"Very few leaders focus on 'the Whole Child' in a variety of settings and make the message and the action stick. Jonathan Raymond has done just that, whether as superintendent of Sacramento Unified or president of the Stuart Foundation. Raymond's book is a relentless call for seeking, serving, and securing the future of all children. What comes through in *Wildflowers* is not only the unwavering commitment to the cause, but what to do about it. Read this book and be both inspired and armed with ideas building a new system of Whole Child support and success."

—Michael Fullan, professor emeritus, OISE/University of Toronto

"Courageously honest, Jonathan Raymond gives us humble and well-needed advice to put down our ideologies and put students and families at the center. This is an important book for those of us who recognize the urgency of transforming education and who want to be engaged in discourse that unites us rather than divides us."

—Gia Truong, CEO, Envision Education

"Raymond takes us on a remarkable leadership journey inside a large urban school district in California's state capitol, Sacramento. His mantra is start with kids and what they need to be successful in the 21st century. Along the way, we encounter his passion and commitment for social and emotional learning, a key feature of any effort to reach the 'Whole Child'—an important acknowledgment that recent past reform efforts have been too narrow in focusing on standardized test scores alone. He brilliantly makes the case that kids have 'heads, hands, and hearts,' and that we must not neglect any aspect of that reality in their learning.

This is a must-read for parents, administrators, teachers, and policy makers who care about children and want the first-hand perspective of a superintendent leader who made a positive difference in improving outcomes for historically underserved students."

—Carl A. Cohn, executive director, California Collaborative for Educational Excellence; former superintendent of Long Beach and San Diego, CA, school systems

"In time of turbulence, disruption, and great uncertainty, few things are more important than a guiding idea. Nowhere is this more so than in education today. From 'high-performing' suburban districts to neglected and underserved urban schools, few students see the purpose in listening to teachers deliver content that they could access online, about subjects unrelated to the challenges of their world, promoting skills for jobs that no longer exist.

"In this stirring book, inspired by the challenges of leading change on the ground, Jonathan Raymond argues that *educating the Whole Child* is just such an idea and that moving beyond lip service demands embracing two critical imperatives: educating the *whole person*—their social, emotional, and cognitive development—and attending to their *whole life*, grounding education in the larger world of family and community beyond school. We mold the future through how we educate our children. What folly to think we can build a society that can address our profound economic, social, and ecological imbalances without making these part of each student's and teacher's journey."

—Peter Senge, MIT Sloan School and J-WEL (Jameel World Education Lab)

"Evidence from many domains—including from education research, psychology, and even neuroscience—points to the social, emotional nature of learning. But what does this mean for those who run America's struggling schools? Drawing from extensive on-the-ground leadership experiences and deep knowledge of child development, Jonathan Raymond deftly illustrates how endemic social issues such as racism and resource inequality impact not only children's learning outcomes but their personal growth, and how leveraging investments in community—school relationships can be game-changing. Rather than proselytizing about "what to do," he masterfully models "how to think," and firmly situates solutions in administrative strategies designed to empower not just the system but the people in it. A must-read for district leaders interested in meaningful change."

—Mary Helen Immordino-Yang, professor of education, psychology & neuroscience, Brain & Creativity Institute, Rossier School of Education, University of Southern California

"Jonathan Raymond clearly reminds us that school reform that does not meet the needs of the Whole Child is not effective or long-lasting. He skillfully points out that feeding the needs of the head, heart, and hands are requirements of a truly powerful and engaging education."

—Peter Gorman, CEO of Peter Gorman Leadership Associates and former superintendent of Charlotte-Mecklenburg Schools in North Carolina

"This is a book about shifting a school system to address the Whole Child. It is an insightful narrative of determination to bring a social-emotional lens to improving learning outcomes for students. This important work makes clear that the way to move our educational system forward is to acknowledge that educational excellence is found at the crossroads of empathy and academic learning."

—Carrie Wilson, executive director, Mills Teacher Scholars of Mills College School of Education

"In his new book, *Wildflowers: A School Superintedent's Challenge to America*, Jonathan Raymond shares his compelling vision for the education of the 'Whole Child.' His clear, concise description of the needs of children, parents, and the entire community is well written and easily understood. He is to be commended for ruffling a few feathers as he calls for structural change in the educational system. It's been my pleasure to know and work with him."

—Tom Payzant, former superintendent, Boston Public Schools

"Jonathan Raymond became the superintendent of Sacramento at the worst of possible times. The severe downturn in our nation's economy drained California's resources used to fund public schools. When money is short, adult dysfunction intensifies, tribal interest groups dig in, and leadership is tested.

"Against the odds, Raymond dramatically grew graduation rates and created 'Priority Schools' to lift expectations and outcomes for kids in historically failing schools. Fueled by daily contact with youth and by his own potentially heartbreaking experience as a young child, Raymond willed change and implemented his vision of creating a 'Whole Child' education for all students.

" *Wildflowers: A School Superintedent's Challenge to America* is a road map on how to create meaningful systemic change. Raymond's time in Sacramento is a case study of leadership facing the toughest of challenges: urban education.

"Prepare to be inspired! Because he did for every kid in Sacramento what wealthier parents require as a matter of course for their children."

—Steve Barr, founder and chairman emeritus, Green Dot Public Schools

"There is a lot of hand-wringing and finger-pointing when it comes to the plight of American K-12 public schools, especially from education partisans, academics, and elected officials. But rarely do we hear the voice of school superintendents who are on the front lines of running our schools. In *Wildflowers: A School Superintedent's Challenge to America*, Jonathan Raymond brings to the table an articulate viewpoint of an urban superintendent worthy of serious consideration. His vision is bold. His successes and lessons learned are well chronicled. His is a fresh perspective on how to systematically improve American schools."

—Gary K. Hart, former California secretary of education

"With *Wildflowers: A School Superintedent's Challenge to America* Jonathan Raymond challenges all of us—parents, community and business leaders, policy makers, and educators—to embrace both academic proficiency and social emotional learning instead of continuing the debate of either/or that defined the No Child Left Behind era. Jonathan makes a compelling case based on his first-person account of transforming learning for students in the Sacramento City Schools as the superintendent of schools. The book is full of inspiring and heart-wrenching stories. It concludes with a call to action and a case study to guide our action. Anyone concerned with educating the Whole Child and the future of education in the 21st century should read *Wildflowers* by Jonathan Raymond."

—Bob Lenz, executive director, Buck Institute for Education

"It is a special treat to find a guide to developing the Whole Child that goes beyond the typical homilies to address the how-to of making it real for students, teachers, superintendents, and communities. This is a practical book and guide derived from the experience of a servant-leader who was a risk-taker and immersed in the community. It is worthy of your time and attention!"

—Joseph M. Patrnchak, author of The Engaged Enterprise; principal, Green Summit Partners LLC; and board chair, Robert Greenleaf Center for Servant-Leadership

"Beautifully written! Jonathan Raymond inspires and challenges all educators to focus and anchor in the true North Star, the Whole Child."

—Ed Manansala, EdD, county superintendent of schools, El Dorado County

"Jonathan Raymond's book, *Wildflowers: A School Superintedent's Challenge to America*, is an important book in the midst of many education books. It is a book that has theory and research, but more importantly, it is all grounded in the real work of a superintendent in a large city. This combination of theory and practice is rare. The book makes ideas come alive with real examples of successes and failures. As Jonathan says, 'I'm telling the truth to myself and the community.'

"The book is not just a case study; there is a vision coming out of the experience with specific ideas for policy makers. I've been an educator for 45 years, and Jonathan's book inspired me and made me look deeper at my own words."

—Dennis Littky, founder, College Unbound

For Sylvie, Joey, and Gabi:
Your curiosity and love of learning inspired me every day to
wake up and fight for kids. I love you!

"And how are the children?"
—Traditional greeting of the Maasai people, Africa

Contents

Foreword

You Had Me at "Whole Child"

I'm thrilled that Jonathan Raymond has written this book and honored to have been asked to reflect on its importance. I am not a classroom educator. My commitment to the Whole Child approach has been realized largely outside of the K-12 education system. The decision to invite comments from someone outside of K-12 education is a testament to Raymond's commitment to "bring community in." This gesture will not go unnoticed by networks and systems of informal educators whose programs, insights, and successes are frequently underutilized in the journey toward the execution of a Whole Child, whole day, whole community vision.

The fact that he invited *me* to comment is evidence that Raymond wants to use his book to help educators understand what it takes to do this sensitively and systemically in ways that can sustain leadership and budget changes. As the "god/grandmother of youth development" (titles I have politely embraced), I am consistently invited to join many K-12-focused discussions of the "nons"—nonacademic, nonschool, noncognitive, noncredit. Once present, I am consistently vocal about two things: 1) there are not only neighborhood organizations, but networks and systems that are organized around these "nons," and 2) their research, practice, and policy expertise could inform, if not accelerate, K-12 innovation. I am not shy. I am sixty-five, black, and female. I have little to lose. I say what I mean.

There are four things that I will say to fellow "noneducators" to encourage them to read this book.

First, Raymond sets a high bar. "Whole Child" is not a catchphrase with youth development professionals. It requires more than the implementation of a checklist of nonacademic services. It is a comprehensive approach, guided by a set of beliefs that requires providers to put children first and accept the responsibility to deliver them at the edge of adulthood not only academically competent, but confident, connected, compassionate, and committed to championing causes bigger than themselves.

Good news: Raymond clears the bar easily with the text. Readers will have so many sections of this book highlighted and underlined and will want to read it twice. This book, more than most books on K-12 education, will give readers a perspective on a) what's possible when a superintendent makes an unflinching commitment to addressing equity through excellence that leads to incredibly difficult decisions, and b) why fulfilling this commitment requires sacrifices, personally and professionally, that in and of themselves may make the less committed look for compromises.

Second, Raymond sets an even higher bar with his goal. "I was also curious about whether we could bring whole-scale improvement to an urban, capital city school district through the application of two objectives: focus on continuous improvement and collaboration, and make every decision from the perspective of what is best for the children."

There are three things that community youth development advocates and practitioners believe in: continuous improvement, collaboration, and putting children first. It is an economic priority. These programs often operate on a shoestring, which means they must collaborate with others to make ends meet, negotiating for everything from space to staff to services. And, while they appreciate research and evidence as much as others, these programs frequently combine elements designed to maximize staff and organizational strengths and address youth and families' needs, which means that efforts to improve are intentionally incremental—building on staff's commit-ment and desire to do better rather than an outsider's insistence that they implement a new curriculum or program model.

Raymond's explanations of how he moved these important ideas into the fabric and flow of the district's work, not through top-down mandates but through listening-driven leadership, bring life to every chapter. His descriptions of how he naturally and strategically incor-porated families, community leaders, and community organizations into the flow will leave readers hungry for more detail. Readers should find ways to use these ideas as springboards for much-needed discussions that cut through rhetoric and focus on the realities of what it takes to innovate and collaborate when scale is the end goal.

Third, Raymond subsumes SEL within the Whole Child mission and ties both to equity. "SEL is Whole Child education in action." He has written a guidebook to making social and emotional learning central to education without once naming an evidence-based SEL curriculum. Instead, he named the strengths he wanted his students to see modeled and built—collaboration, creativity, critical thinking, compassion, empathy—and the supplemental subjects and settings in which they often build them (music and art, after school, and sum-mer learning opportunities). He writes frequently and fluently about the need to give "disadvantaged children access to music and dance, stimulating classwork, summer learning opportunities, family support, and other services." His conviction that subjects such as music and art and settings such as after school and summer are inherently "SEL rich" provides fertile ground for facilitating discussions between K-12 and ecosystem leaders and practitioners that can go beyond "where and when" learning happens to explore "how and why" it happens, especially for poor students and students of color.

Equally impressive, he has written a story about how he pursued equity for the poorest students in his district without ever saying the word. He has done this by showing that when districts priori-tize Whole Child excellence, they "nurture the sense of safety and self-confidence that some call persistence and productive struggle, and that children raised in poverty—regardless of race—often have a challenging time developing at home" and demonstrating that, when this goal is accomplished, test scores rise.

Fourth, in explaining why innovations within the K-12 system often fail to scale, he helps readers understand why efforts outside the system often fail to be seen. His powerful, personal story will help readers see how he encouraged nonprofit partners to fit fully into a district-wide effort to "focus on the Whole Child—head, heart, and hands—as well as on the family and community." He names individual nonprofits (e.g., the Parent Teacher Home Visit Project) that supported this work and discusses programs and initiatives that were made possible because of partnerships with business, foundation, and public agency leaders. Raymond doesn't, however, go out of his way to discuss the systems or structures behind these leaders.

I know, for example, that Sacramento, like many other cities, has out-of-school time intermediaries that work with programs such as the Men's Leadership Academy to help them improve the quality and reach of their programming. So why weren't they featured? Because in the end, it was Raymond's responsibility to figure out how to scale these ideas and innovations to meet the needs of more students. And, as each response to a challenge makes clear, it was his job to look for and nurture these ideas and innovations within the staff, the schools, the families, and the community's nonprofits, businesses, foundations, and public agencies.

He could have taken the easy route and picked one. He didn't. He could have waited for proposals and offers to come to him. He didn't. Jonathan hit the streets and talked to youth, families, teachers, and leaders on the ground. He worked to bring the best of what he found to scale as quickly as he could. That meant bringing a brilliantly effective community leader, such as Koua Jacklyn Franz, former executive director of the Hmong Women's Heritage Association, onto his team as his chief family and community engagement officer. Sometimes it meant bucking the Teacher's Union to ensure that the innovative whole school models, like the Waldorf model, could step out from the shadows and be recognized and acknowledged by the system as alternatives to the status quo. Sometimes it meant finding outside funding to take good ideas, such as Parent Resource Centers to scale with community partners.

But at every turn, Jonathan was driven appropriately by a commitment to managing structural change in a massive, multidimensional system. He learned over the course of his tenure with the Sacramento City Unified School District that he would have to plan and implement with the end in mind. Piecemeal solutions (e.g., drawing all the best teachers to the Priority Schools) have unintended consequences. Readers will learn, over the course of studying Jonathan's story, that stakeholders have to meet each other halfway. They must be prepared to show district leaders that they are not only willing collaborators, but prepared, responsible, and successful stewards of the Whole Child vision. And, like the teachers from the Waldorf school who self-funded their training, waiting for their moment to innovate from within, they have to believe that leaders such as Jonathan are looking for real partners, not just available volunteers.

After reading this book, I'm ready to partner and to bring my friends with me.

—*Karen Pittman, president, The Forum for Youth Investment,*

Introduction

From August 2009 through December 2013, I had the honor of serving as superintendent of the Sacramento City Unified School District (SCUSD), the eleventh-largest school district in the state of California. This book describes my four-and-a-half-year experience leading a public school system where nearly three-quarters of the families served have incomes below the federal poverty threshold, in a district whose residents speak more than forty different languages.

My purpose in writing this book, put simply, is to inspire change. By telling the story of my Sacramento journey—what I learned, where I succeeded and where I failed, the structural problems I encountered, and the innovative solutions my team applied—I aim to issue a challenge to every American concerned with public education to rethink their views and actions.

Whether you are a parent, educator, school administrator or school board member, a funder or an education advocate, this book represents a challenge to relinquish dogma and ideology and reframe the endless debate over public education through the perspective that matters most: that of our children. Only when we begin to align around this critical viewpoint can we hope to end the debate and finally advance the field.

Could this ever really happen? I know it can. Because it's what happened to me. After arriving in Sacramento full of aspirations shaped by my training and preparation, I came face-to face-with the realities of the lives of my 47,000 students and found myself seeking new and different solutions to the daily problems confronting our stressed and underfunded district.

I can proudly tell you many of these solutions had a lasting effect. As reported by EdSource, California's foremost resource for information about its schools, I departed Sacramento with "a credible list of accomplishments at least partly attributable to [my] leadership,"[1] including "greatly expanded summer programs, new college and career programs tied to businesses and the community, home-school visits and new parent-teacher partnerships," along with a "new focus on social and emotional aspects of learning."[2]

The district-wide graduation rate, which was 68 percent when I arrived, rose each year of my tenure, hitting the 85 percent mark the year of my departure. Described as a "hard-charging leader"[3] by *The Sacramento Bee*, I undeniably ruffled some feathers. But it's not a boast to say the numbers speak for themselves, and I'm especially proud that graduation rates rose in particular for our most challenged students, including those tracked as socioeconomically disadvantaged, special ed, and English learners, who alone constituted one-quarter of the student body.

Of course, no account of confronting a challenge is useful if failure is left unexamined. As someone who studies and aspires to leader-

---

[1] John Fensterwald, "Taking stock of Jonathan Raymond's tenure and legacy at Sac City," EdSource, December 21, 2003, https://edsource.org/2013/taking-stock-of-jonathan-raymonds-tenure-and-legacy-at-sac-city/54013.

[2] Ibid.

[3] Loretta Kalb, "Fresno school administrator tapped as new chief for Sacramento City Unified," The Sacramento Bee, April 18, 2017, http://www.sacbee.com/news/local/education/article145321159.html.

ship, I believe in telling the truth to myself and my community. Perhaps Sacramento's greatest lesson—and one I could only fully grasp in hindsight—is that taking on problems one at a time will inevitably cause different problems to erupt when the issues you're trying to solve lay nested in a massive bureaucratic system. Sacramento made me a believer in structural change because in an intricate, multilayered system like a school district, every small decision triggers a cascade of unintended consequences and controversies.

No doubt my most controversial project was what we termed the Superintendent's Priority Schools, in which our lowest-performing campuses were literally transformed from the inside out. Despite the conflicts they created, the Priority Schools stand as a microcosm of what can be accomplished when risks are taken for kids and when grown-ups act like grown-ups by working collaboratively and creatively on behalf of the children and families they serve.

You may notice that I frequently refer to families, and not just children, when I speak about the people who are served by public schools. That's intentional! In the chapters that follow, as you accompany me on my journey as superintendent, you will learn how valuable and necessary it is for public schools to treat education as a service to the entire community and not just its youth. It is imperative that we seek out and engage all stakeholders and contributors who help improve good schools and turn struggling schools around. You will discover, as I did, that the key to effectively educating children is to focus on the Whole Child—head, heart, and hands—as well as on the family and community.

The Whole Child approach you will read about is not some new age trend—it's a deeply established, road-tested, outcome-focused approach that influences every aspect of our children's educational experience. In fact, as you'll learn in chapter two, our country's public school system was founded on Whole Child values from the start. There is widespread lack of understanding about what Whole Child education is, and perhaps it helps to ask the question differently: How do schools, classrooms, and communities support the Whole Child? Our education system must reflect what parents and families inherently know about what it takes for their kids to be "whole"—happy, healthy, connected, and learning.

Once you've read how Sacramento's students, families, teachers, and communities benefitted and grew thanks to Whole Child thinking, I hope you will agree that our country's prospects will improve if every community adopted a Whole Child focus. Indeed, had our current leaders benefited from this approach in their own educations, America would be further along in the quest for excellent education and less arrested by ideological clashes and chronic underfunding.

I learned so much as superintendent. Though my time in Sacramento was in many ways exhausting and even heartbreaking, it left me with a greater-than-ever passion and commitment to forging ahead with the changes needed to ensure a rewarding future for all our kids. Sir Ken Robinson said it best: "The gardener does not make a plant grow. The job of a gardener is to create optimal conditions." I hope that by sharing my experience, I will inspire you to share my passion. Having learned the hard lessons of trying to solve individual problems that were embedded in a massive, multidimensional system, I hope you'll understand why I call for structural change—to create the optimal conditions for children to thrive. I hope you'll share my deep certainty that a better future for our children is an attainable goal. Whether we get there in the end rests with you, with me, with all of us as a nation.

Why I Am Challenging America

Nearly five years in Sacramento gave me first-hand insight into the problems and solutions our country must engage to make good on its promises of innovation, opportunity, equality, and success. I can say with certainty that our public schools have never held more potential. Every day, I saw children excel against the odds. I saw parents strive to protect and empower their families to ensure a bright future. I saw teachers, principals, and other educators leave it all in the classroom and the school in support of their students. And, with equal certainty, I can say that we're reaching a tipping point.

While education policy experts argue over approaches and legislators horse-trade over funds, our country creeps toward decline through the abject neglect of our children. Are your children exempt because they're in private school? Don't kid yourself. Our nation has one future to build, together. Nothing will shield us from the consequences if we fail those on the lower rungs of our economic ladder.

The aim of these pages is to take you on the same journey that my years in Sacramento took me: a journey that will challenge your beliefs and values, show you some successful approaches to K-12 education, transmit the urgency of acting now, and inspire you to believe in change and in the remarkable potential of our children. I hope to imbue you with a vision of the excellence and greatness our schools, our communities, and our country are capable of if we do right by our children.

Is it impossible? Absolutely not. Reshaping public education is the opposite of impossible. It's consistent with our history and character as Americans and a realistic and achievable goal. Above all, it's a goal we can and must reach together in the spirit of community. My time as superintendent and the years of reflection that followed have committed me irrevocably to this mission. If we join together, we can catalyze a breakthrough moment in public education, one in which we move beyond the one-size-fits-all, industrial model of instruction to a fully enlightened, progressive climate of learning for all.

Prologue

My Journey to California

"Look to the hills boys, look to the hills. Finish strong, boys, finish strong." — Frank L. Boyden

The Path to My New Career

My new position as superintendent capped nearly a decade of professional involvement with kids and education. I began as president of the Commonwealth Corporation in Boston, which focused on developing support systems for at-risk and out-of-school youth as well as job-training programs. But my personal stake in disrupting the education system's status quo dates back much, much further.

I was a sixth grader when my parents received a call from my school's principal proposing they place me back in the fifth grade. I wasn't reading at grade level, they were told, probably because of a learning disability. Fortunately for me, my mother had been trained as a teacher and knew to dig deeper than the conclusions the school had reached.

Instead of sending me back to fifth grade, my parents sent me to a psychologist. What followed was two days of testing and the best learning experience I'd had thus far! The psychologist concluded that far from being disabled, I was bored and needed to be pushed. His prescription was a more challenging and structured learning environment. This was my first encounter with the realities of a system in which the fate of a child is never secure. Without my mother's dogged advocacy, I would have been held back, possibly tracked into special education, and most definitely not encouraged to live up to my full potential.

Thanks to my mom's persistence, I soon got to experience the other side of the educational coin: a truly inspiring teacher, who—years before the specialists began talking about Whole Child education—understood instinctively that a child's intellect and success are inseparable from his or her spirit and emotions. Harry Boyadjian, whose survival of the Armenian genocide certainly informed his insight into the human psyche, taught geography at my new school. I arrived midway through the year, always a challenging situation for a young student.

Mr. Boyadjian's geography classroom was full of maps, and as he walked around the room pointing to various places, he would tell stories that made the cities and countries come to life. My first test earned me a seventy-three, yet Mr. Boyadjian praised and encouraged me: "You weren't even in my class for a week and you had to take a test!" he marveled, putting his hand on my shoulder. "What a great job you did! You even knew where Mesopotamia is." Instead of feeling ashamed, I felt encouraged and successful.

I entered his class thinking geography was all about rocks. By the time I left, I had the emotional resilience to confidently discuss geography with my peers and the empathy to wonder how it related to the world news my parents talked about over dinner. His arm on my shoulder that first week in a new school shaped my own destiny of putting my arms around as many children as I could, helping them believe in themselves and feel as special and accomplished as Mr. Boyadjian made me feel.

During the winter of my senior year in high school, I worked in Boston's South End as a fourth-grade student teacher. Most days I'd do whatever the teacher asked: get supplies, help take the children to lunch, or make "steno" copies. How I loved the smell of that blue ink! Then one day I was paired with Edwin, who, like me just a few years earlier, wasn't reading at grade level. My job was to sit and read with him for thirty minutes a day. At first, I was doing all the reading. Edwin was shy. But as he grew more comfortable with me, he started to try. Part of a sentence here, a portion of a paragraph there, and gradually Edwin was doing most of the work himself.

It's not so much that I taught him to read: Edwin taught himself, once somebody took an interest and believed in him—perhaps before he believed in himself. That's what gave him the confidence to trust and try. The smile in his eyes that greeted me every day has never left my mind. As I think back now, it was Edwin who connected me back to my own sixth-grade self and brought to life the urgency of reaching more children.

Perhaps that's why almost twenty years later, with a career in law and politics behind me, I found myself at the Commonwealth Corporation supporting disadvantaged children. While the nonprofit was helping hundreds of young people throughout Massachusetts, I longed to have a larger effect—particularly in urban areas where, for all but a few children, the road to a better life runs through our public school system.

Around Labor Day of 2005, I happened to hear about the Broad Academy in two separate meetings. I applied to the program—a ten-month fellowship preparing experienced professionals to serve as urban superintendents—and was fortunate to be accepted. Following my time with Broad, I spent nearly three years as chief accountability officer for the Charlotte-Mecklenburg Schools, a district run by an amazing superintendent and his talented team. This confirmed my interest in leading an urban school district, and when the 2009 school year began for the Sacramento City Unified School District, I found myself at its helm.

Charlotte, North Carolina
October 2007

One day after school, my first-grade daughter Sylvie, who was learning how to read, picked up my business card and asked, "Daddy, what does a chief accountability officer do?" I was working in Charlotte at the time, and in a *How the Grinch Stole Christmas*–like moment, I responded, "Honey, my job is to catch people doing good things." I didn't realize it at the time, but these simple words that I believed in represented a major shift from the punitive accountability frame of No Child Left Behind. Characterized by high-stakes testing based on a set of academic standards, No Child Left Behind was proving to be ineffective as a federal education policy lever. At best, the legislation punished the very children it was designed to support, while at worst it incentivized cheating. Clearly, we needed another way. The work we began doing in Charlotte—providing educators with data and information on student performance, providing resources to improve instruction, and finding the right balance of pressure to drive improvement—was working.

In 2011, Charlotte-Mecklenburg Schools received the prestigious Broad Prize for excellence in urban education. Certainly, the culture of continuous improvement we started building during my time contributed. I wondered what could happen to advance children's learning if I were ever a superintendent and used a theory of change, as Sir Ken Robinson describes in *Creative Schools*, that was based on getting people to work together and focus on getting a bit better every day.

But I learned something more important that formed the foundation for my belief in Whole Child education. When Sylvie came home from her first day as a first-grader, she burst into tears.

"What's wrong, honey?" I asked.

"Allie's not in my class this year," she said through her tears. Sylvie's former classmate, in a wheelchair from an early age, was part of her kindergarten class, an inclusive class where children with disabilities learn in the classroom alongside their peers. The class was co-taught by a regular education teacher and a special-education teacher. Research and data show that such an approach enables all students to thrive. More importantly, it teaches children empathy, compassion, and tolerance. Sylvie missed her friend, whom she wheeled to lunch and played with during recess. What Sylvie reminded her mother and me of that day would later help inform the Whole Child approach that blossomed in Sacramento.

Becoming an urban superintendent was a dream that came later in life for me. I was fortunate that this dream-come-true opportunity came for me in the late summer of 2009 in Sacramento, California. So began the journey from No Child to Whole Child.

Sacramento, California
August 2009

Shortly after I arrived in California to lead the Sacramento City Unified School District, *The Sacramento Bee* published a cartoon of me in a clean white apron, holding a mop and bucket, poised by a doorway marked "SCUSD." Through the open doorway was a schoolroom utterly in shambles, as if ravaged by a hurricane.

No wonder. Upon my arrival as a recently minted graduate of the Broad Academy, California ranked forty-seventh out of fifty states in per-pupil spending, forty-ninth in the number of guidance counselors per student (one counselor for every 810 students), and dead last in the number of K-12 students per teacher.

As a relative newcomer to the field of education, I had expected my learning curve to be steep, but no one—not my Academy instructors, not my coaches and mentors, not my family, not my fellow graduates—could have predicted the full scope of what lay before me. Had I deliberately set out to immerse myself in the fiercest and most important conflicts over public education in twenty-first-century America, I couldn't have timed my arrival better.

My new school district was in its sixth straight year of budget cuts. Besides the devastating effects of the Great Recession combined with the lasting effects of Prop 13, the district was seeing its student population shrink—the result both of California's plummeting birthrate and of young families fleeing a deteriorating school system, provided they had the means to do so.

Of course, for the families who remained in Sacramento, the "shrinkage"—which was so vivid to policy makers—was a mere abstraction. Their reality was their 47,000 children, who were seeking and who deserved a first-rate education, and who had needs as varied as you'd expect in "America's Most Diverse City" (so designated by *Time* magazine in 2002). Nearly 75 percent of SCUSD students lived at or below the federal poverty line and qualified for free or reduced lunch. Twenty percent were nonnative English speakers. Like many urban school systems, the district struggled with large achievement gaps and a general sense among the citizenry that struggling schools, like poverty, were an immovable fact of life.

As a one-time Republican congressional candidate, I'm not a guy inclined to think throwing money at a problem is the best way to fix it. Stepping into a position with a $400 million budget, my intent was to improve both the business strategy (educating and developing children) and the operations strategy (improving services and supports to schools and families). I was also curious whether we could bring whole-scale improvement to an urban, capital city school district though two objectives: continuous improvement and collaboration, and decision-making from the perspective of what is best for the children.

Indeed, our school district credo became "Putting Children First." Easy words to say, for sure, but could we actually live by this in everything we did? Were we successful? Yes and no. While I'll readily take credit for my achievements and responsibility for my shortcomings, I learned in my four-and-a-half-year tenure that the systemic issues we face in public education are far too great for any one man, woman, or policy to fix. What are these issues? Every education advocate will have his or her own list, and mine includes:

- misuse of data and accountability to punish teachers and students

- exclusion of parents and the community from decision-making

- scant and/or misdirected funding

- lack of vision and messaging

- cynicism about the potential of our young people

- rigid, outdated, and irrelevant curricula

- high-stakes testing that fails to assess the true capabilities of students

- forgetting the importance of relationships among students, teachers, and families, and

- not putting students at the center of the work

Make no mistake: these issues must be viewed in the context of a public education system segregated by class and race, with our most vulnerable and disadvantaged children receiving an unequal share of resources. Americans seem to have a tough time thinking through problems that involve inequality. Wherever it crops up, people reach for their pet ideologies before even agreeing on the facts.

That is exactly why we need a new approach to public education, one that puts down ideology and doesn't take sides except for taking the side of children. We need to reject the "either/or model" that picks winners and losers. Instead, we must access our ability to approach a challenge from a "both/and" perspective, a framework of mutual respect and compromise. Every child and adult in America will continue to pay a price until we do what we call on our children to do daily: learn from our mistakes, and find a new way forward.

Chapter 1

Man Meets Sacramento

Putting Down the Baggage

As a graduate of the Broad Academy, I arrived in Sacramento knowing I'd have my detractors. Founded by billionaire businessman and philanthropist Eli Broad, the Academy trains senior-level executives from a range of fields, including education, to lead urban school districts beset with systemic challenges. For some, this is controversial. While the Academy's supporters point to the ability of its graduates to bring about much-needed change, critics charge it imposes an unwelcome corporate mindset on public schools. Some even denounce its graduates as emissaries of privatization, committed to replacing public education with charter schools.

My four-and-a-half years in Sacramento taught me once and for all that the greatest danger to our nation's public education system is ideology. Poverty and racial segregation may be its most immediate challenges, but if we stay mired in ideologically driven battles (e.g., charter schools, vouchers, etc.) at the district, state, and federal levels, no substantial progress can be made to tackle the chronic underfunding, aging infrastructure, lack of ownership by students and educators alike, and misguided policies that trap too many children in achievement, opportunity, and belief gaps.

Is better management the answer? Sure, it's a piece of the puzzle. Over time, every type of organization gets comfortable with its own inefficiencies. This is true for businesses and nonprofits, government agencies, and sports teams. It's also true of schools and school districts. When the future of our children is on the line, we must be impatient with their inefficiencies, their entrenched habits, and all the barriers to progress that accumulate within organizations like dust gathering under a sofa. When it comes to educating and developing children, we can't accept that good is good enough.

I arrived in Sacramento determined to change the school district's culture by putting children at the center of every single decision, focusing on getting a little bit better at what we did every day, and setting aside our personal agendas to work together. Outsiders like I was lack the years of shared experiences that many traditional educators have in common, and perhaps that's the point: it takes a newcomer with fresh eyes to ask new questions. One question I asked each time I visited a school and classroom was: Would I want one of my three children to be in this classroom? It's amazing how this simple question kept me moving forward during even the toughest and most challenging days.

In his classic book on leadership, *The Path of Least Resistance*, former musical composer Robert Fritz asserts that altering behaviors and outcomes requires a focus not on the behaviors themselves, but on the underlying structures in which they reside. He compares organizations to rivers. Changing the direction of a river requires changing the rocks and boulders in the riverbed.

If we want to reshape how schools and school districts are managed and perform—if we seek to change behavior—it's the underlying structures we must change. This doesn't mean an arrogant, top-down dictatorship. In fact, often it's about encouraging leadership from the bottom up by listening. Great leadership means humility, not arrogance. It means having empathy and compassion for the children you serve and colleagues you work with. It means having a sense of what it's like to walk in the shoes of those in your school's community. It means suspending judgment and practicing self-awareness.

That was how I arrived in Sacramento, eager to make a positive difference for kids and committed to partnering with my new colleagues and respecting their wisdom and experience.

Two strengths helped me transition smoothly: my Broad Academy training and support, and my personality. Broad equipped me with the right antenna and offered ongoing coaching. I arrived in a state of high awareness about what to look for, think about, and question.

The Academy didn't push me out of the plane and watch to see if the parachute opened. Instead, I got quarterly visits from my Academy mentor, Tom Payzant, former superintendent of the San Diego and Boston public school systems, one-time assistant secretary of education, and professor at Harvard's Graduate School of Education. Tom's coaching was invaluable as I absorbed the realities of my new responsibilities. In the moments when I felt overwhelmed—and such moments weren't rare—I remembered his most valuable advice: "Being a school superintendent means knowing what to do when you don't know what to do."

Though Broad in no way prepared me for the sheer intensity of the job or the urgency of creating trusting relationships with the teachers, principals, parents, and students making up my new community, on some level I knew, instinctively, how to make my way.

A couple of my earliest decisions helped offset the natural skepticism of lifelong educators about an outsider in their midst. First, when my family and I moved to Sacramento, I sent my children—ages seven, six, and two—to our public schools. Notably, I was the first superintendent in twenty-five years to put my own kids in the system I was running, and that sent a signal to everyone in the community.

Second, I hit the streets. My message to the community was: *I'll talk to anyone willing to give me five minutes of their time—just don't come to my office, because I won't be there!* Every day, I visited a different school campus, district facility, community center, or student's home. I arrived with no entourage and no driver. One afternoon, when I dropped in unannounced on a teacher whose class had just left for the day, she threw her arms around me and thanked me for coming around like a normal guy doing his job, not like a big shot. That sent a signal, too.

During my first one hundred days, the people of Sacramento saw me everywhere, talking to everyone, asking questions. I wanted to understand their hopes and dreams for their children and our community, how we could improve education in Sacramento, and what advice they would have for me as their new superintendent.

One young pregnant mother gave the best advice I could have asked for, saying, "Superintendent, take risks for kids." A Hmong community elder said, "Those in positions to make change must make change." With California schools ranked among the worst in the nation, disrupting the *status quo* was an imperative, not an option.

Hiring My Team

Among my excursions during my first one hundred days was a visit to the Hmong Women's Heritage Association, a nonprofit seeking to improve the prospects for Hmong youth through mentoring, after-school programs and other interventions. California has the second-largest Hmong community in the United States, with Fresno and Sacramento as its epicenters. Among the most recent Asian immigrants to America, the Hmong are refugees who worked with American troops during the Vietnam War and came here in its aftermath. Their youth confront issues such as an academic achievement gap and racial stereotyping.

Executive Director Koua Jacklyn Franz was blunt with me. When I shared my vision of a system centered around the child, her response was, "As superintendent, can you make real decisions?" I answered in the affirmative, and she said, "Then please make decisions."

With tears in her eyes, she explained to me that it wasn't her own children she worried about. As an educated professional, she could fight for her kids. "You must make decisions," Koua said, "on behalf of the children who don't have a voice, whose parents don't speak English, or fear speaking to officials, or work late into the night."

Her passion was immediately apparent. The child of refugees herself, Koua considered education the key driver for the advancement of her community. Raised in Sacramento, she returned there after college, determined to serve her community and help it rise. In her, I saw the concerns of every marginalized parent: "How can I make my children matter to a massive bureaucracy that is deeply attached to one-way directives and top-down decision-making, that prioritizes standardization instead of customized lesson plans, that clings to outdated assumptions about who can and cannot learn, and that treats schools like locked fortresses, not neighborhood centers for community growth?"

What she said hit me right where I lived: the child without a voice is why superintendents must truly lead, must not be passive, must make the affirmative choice to stop perpetuating inequality. After we'd talked for a while, she explained she had a meeting to host. Representatives from the Sacramento Police Department were coming to her office to discuss problems with racial profiling of Hmong youth. She expected me to leave. Instead, I asked to sit in. As the new superintendent, I needed to be there.

I think I surprised her, but she invited me to stay. As the meeting progressed, I witnessed first-hand how our community was divided and conflicted, how bureaucracy and competing agendas distract people from the kids at the center of the equation, how the *status quo* feeds off the inertia of adults unwilling to take risks. I also witnessed how far Koua was willing to go to interrupt those cycles, and when the meeting ended and her visitors left, I surprised her again.

"Would you come work for me?" I asked.

That moment perfectly models my hiring philosophy. Koua didn't come from the field of education; she came from the community I was charged with serving. In her I saw strength, intelligence, experience with children's issues, and a deep commitment to change. But, as the song goes, you can't always get what you want. My first job offer to Koua was met with a flat "no." She already had her dream job, representing her community.

Eventually, we compromised. Koua—who later would serve as my chief family and community engagement officer—agreed to consult for SCUSD. In that capacity, she guided the creation of our strategic plan. Its title said everything: Putting Children First. Its anchors were three foundational pillars:

1. Career- and College-Ready Students

2. Family and Community Engagement

3. Organizational Transformation

The origins of the plan, as well as its content, represent the mark I sought to make on Sacramento: leadership that comes not from the inside out, but from the outside in. The district's strategic plan came literally from the community, not from district insiders isolated from the realities of the lives we wanted to affect.

In crafting the document, Koua consulted with community partners such as students, teachers, administrators, parents, colleges, businesses, and local nonprofits. Some of the key programs we went on to introduce, like our robust home visits and our welcoming schools, had already been on her radar through her work with the Hmong community.

Before my arrival, the head of the Broad Academy, Tim Quinn, had told me I'd be doing well if I had my senior team in place by the end of my first year. *Wow,* I'd thought at the time, *a full year? How could I wait that long?* Soon, I knew Tim had been right. Building a team takes time. Unlike many superintendents, I resisted the urge to import my entire staff from outside the school district.

Instead, I looked for people in the community, professionals who brought a new perspective and fresh eyes—like Koua, and like our chief of communications, Gabe Ross. Both had deep connections to the local community, though they had never worked in public education. I also promoted many talented veterans of the school system, like Stacey Bell, Teresa Cummings, and Patty Hagemeyer, into leadership roles and made sure their talents weren't diverted into serving the district bureaucracy instead of the children.

We had stars and talent everywhere. I just had to be patient and seek it out. I'm amazed and chagrined when I hear stories of superintendents coming into their new districts and bringing in dozens of folks from outside the community. In the end, superintendents come and go. A superintendent's enduring legacies are the people and the structural change they're able to achieve. Such change must be grounded in a shared vision, so it can't be easily dislodged on the whim of a school board or a new trend in education. What matters are the folks who stay behind to carry on the work and the tools you leave for them in the form of a vision strong enough to sustain the changes made.

Have you planted the sparks in their hearts? Have you inspired and opened their minds to what is possible? In the end, what will make the difference are the opportunities a superintendent offers people on the ground, the vision that's built in collaboration with them, and the changes deeply rooted in that vision. Enabling residents with local roots to serve children and affect change is one of the greatest things a superintendent can do.

Facing the Challenge of Poverty

At the start of my first school year in Sacramento, I was part of a group of school superintendents and elected officials who met with US Secretary of Education Arne Duncan. He reminded us that California—whose 2008 public school performance got a D-minus from *Education Week*—was educating a full one-eighth of the nation's students. As leaders, we had to do better by our youth, and for me, how we educated our most disadvantaged kids was our most urgent challenge.

The impact of poverty on education is an entrenched problem in California and throughout the country. Policymakers call it the "achievement" or "opportunity gap," but I use these terms with grave hesitation. First reported in 1966, the "achievement gap" refers to demographic variances among children in academic performance. Yes, my new district struggled with disparities in performance between white students and students of color, between students just learning English and native English speakers, between poor kids and children from more prosperous homes, and between regular-education students and those with disabilities.

But the pitfalls of the "achievement gap" rhetoric have outstripped the term's usefulness. While education reform efforts like the No Child Left Behind Act claimed to attack the so-called "achievement gap" head on, many of the vestiges of this policy, such as high-stakes testing, only contribute to perpetuating the "gap." What do I mean by this?

Because of high-stakes testing and the "all or nothing," "pass or fail" frame of No Child Left Behind, the kids who most need to experience success rarely get that opportunity. They could achieve two years of academic growth in a single year, but still be designated a failure if they don't score high enough on a standardized test! How does this reinforce a sense of accomplishment in students, and in the educators working tirelessly to support them?

During my tenure in Sacramento, I observed another frustrating pitfall of focusing on the "gap" when I visited the Jeremiah E. Burke High School in Boston, a notorious "drop-out factory" targeted for improvement under No Child Left Behind.

Federal funds from a three-year grant allowed the school to add a range of new counseling programs, support systems, and teacher training which indeed improved student performance in objective, measurable ways. But if you're targeting a "gap," your only goal is to close the "gap," not to find ways for children to feel and experience success, not to promote continuous improvement for educators, and not to build collaborative, empathetic school cultures.

So, after three years of steady gains in test scores, Jeremiah E. Burke lost the essential programs and services that had so nurtured its students because as test scores rose, the "gap" narrowed. Mission accomplished? How absurd! The Burke school showed me that the resources needed to educate young people living in poverty are necessities, not luxuries or extras. That's part of the reason I reject the term "achievement gap," and instead talk about the effects of poverty and the power of belief. A lack of belief in children isn't solved by short-term fixes, and neither are the challenges of students living in poverty.

I also reject the term because it implicitly blames children who live in poverty for the failures of policy makers and so-called "experts" in education. Who is failing to achieve? The students who are underperforming, or the adults who lack the focus, discipline, moral courage, and belief in these kids to ensure they are supported effectively?

Back in 1966, with legal segregation barely in the rearview mirror, the average African-American high school senior was found to score in the thirteenth percentile in both reading and math, behind 87 percent of white students. As recent studies show, this disparity has barely shifted, a fact that Eric Hanushek of the Hoover Institution at Stanford calls "a national embarrassment." An embarrassment, yes, but hardly a surprise when you consider the movement to integrate schools peaked in 1988. That year, the difference in reading scores between black and white students had dropped by 50 percent. In the ensuing years, as schools resegregated, that difference grew again.

Today, in a major metropolitan area like New York City, 85 percent of African-American children and 75 percent of their Latino peers attend schools that are considered intensely segregated, i.e., less than 10 percent of students are white. Sacramento was similar. While about 19 percent of students in the overall district were white, they tended to cluster in schools where the white population was higher. Overall, California schools lead the nation in racial segregation, from its major cities to its suburbs.

The most significant factor in performance disparities, however, isn't race, but socioeconomic status. We don't like to discuss class differences in America, but fifty years of research have confirmed it: The most effective solution to the so-called achievement gap is sending children to schools with a broad mix of rich and poor, blue collar and white collar, working class and the one percent.

In Charlotte, where I worked before Sacramento, the city's desegregation efforts mixed working-class black children with middle-class white children. There was also a widespread and successful campaign to involve parents from both communities in their children's education. This thoughtful and complex effort—class-conscious desegregation combined with community involvement—yielded gains in achievement unmatched in districts that simply bussed kids from poor black neighborhoods into poor white ones and failed to engage the families affected by the program.

The effects of poverty on a child's academic performance are as varied as they are well-documented: emotional trauma, household insta-
bility, and lack of access to health care are just a few of the pressures
that interfere with learning. The comforts and supports more affluent
families take for granted—stimulating books and toys, exposure to
the arts, enriching summer experiences, and quality time with rested
parents who aren't working multiple jobs—reinforce a child's sense
of safety, self-confidence, and resilience. That social and emotional
well-being, in turn, enables strong scholastic achievement.

Yet disadvantaged kids are not doomed to failure—far from it. While I
couldn't wave a wand and make it rain gold coins in Sacramento's low-income communities, I did have one valuable tool at my disposal. It
wasn't a lesson plan, a checklist, or a policy paper, but rather a strong
belief in all children, and in schools that tend to the Whole Child.

Chapter 2

The Whole Child in Context

The Whole Child and the Issue of Class

By giving our disadvantaged children access to music and dance, stimulating classwork, summer learning opportunities, family support, and other services, we nurtured that sense of safety and self-confidence that some call persistence and productive struggle, and which children raised in poverty — regardless of race — often have a challenging time developing at home.

That's why we focused on excellence and giving our students and families opportunities to choose from a portfolio of schools, including high-performing charter schools. I remember being asked at one of my first community meetings how I felt about charter schools. I responded that I like charter schools that work for kids and families. If our schools weren't getting the job done (and clearly in extreme poverty areas such as Oak Park and parts of South Sacramento, we were not), then parents should have other options. I viewed our charter schools as healthy competition and places we should be learning from and with.

When charter schools are integrated and share best practices and partner with district schools, they can help lift entire neighborhoods. In fact, within a few years of my arrival, Oak Park, with its mix of charter and district schools and the culture of communication and trust we established, had some of Sacramento's best schools in both categories.

We also expanded successful programs with long waiting lists of students, such as our integrated thematic and Waldorf schools. Then we created new programs, such as Chinese and Hmong language immersion, college and career pathways, and a pre-K-12 International Baccalaureate program.

In addition to more school choices for families, we took a Whole Child approach to our calendar, extending the school day and school year for our children. After-school programs were expanded, and we brought more providers into our communities to improve the quality of these programs and increase their offerings. We learned that expanded learning programs (i.e., after-school and summer), with their focus on creating safe and engaging cultures, helped teach our young people empathy and compassion.

The Whole Child is about educating the heart and the hand as well as the head. It is about enabling children to believe in them-selves, to know they have a voice, to know they can create, to have a sense of belonging, and to know and say out loud what excites them, challenges them, and scares them. It means championing empathy and compassion, feeding our kids food that is nutritious, and offering dental and medical care to kids whose families can't.

Our children come to school with so many needs. We must meet them where they are, give them a say, and listen to their voices. We must encourage flexible thinking and emotional intelligence. Seeing each child as a whole human being—not just a mind for testing—is core to my philosophy of education.

Whole Child education was not part of the Broad curriculum, though it should have been. Any superintendent who sees the challenges children face daily in high poverty districts must conclude that "education" is about more than test scores. Any thinking human being who sees them would reach the same conclusion.

The day my kids came home from their new Sacramento school and said, "Dad, did you know they serve corn dogs for breakfast?," I realized my responsibilities extended far outside the classroom. My visit to Jeremiah E. Burke had only strengthened my sense that our focus on the Whole Child must be bold and unwavering.

That sense was also confirmed the day I took part in "Challenge Day" at one of our high schools, particularly in an exercise called "Crossing the Line." As we stood together on one side of a room, a moderator called out, "Cross the line if you've seen a crime on your street; cross the line if someone you love died violently; cross the line if you know an alcoholic." As child after child stepped to the other side of the room, I realized what a great victory it was for them to even show up to school.

Are skills such as creativity, collaboration, critical thinking, and communication important for our kids? Absolutely. Equally important is helping our kids develop empathy and compassion, and modeling those qualities for them. Our kids are extraordinary, yet we barely know the challenges and pressures they face. Once they got to school, it was up to us, the adults in our system and community, to ensure that they could learn and feel safe, secure, and cared for, whether that meant adding satellite health centers to our campuses, leadership programs, or gardens to grow nutritious food.

SEL: Whole Child Education in Action

While the district's new commitment to expanded learning gave our kids important skills to help them master academic content, it also modeled and accelerated our efforts to bring social and emotional learning (SEL) into the school day.

What is SEL? I would call it *Whole Child education in action*, assisting educators and students alike to focus on the Whole Child through an approach to learning that emphasizes inquiry, understanding, genuine caring and compassion for each other, deep listening, collaboration, and active engagement with classroom and world topics. SEL also aims to strengthen emotional resilience and social skills, two key factors to success both in school and in life. [4]

If you've ever sat in a meeting wondering why you're there, what it's about, and whether you or the person at the whiteboard could use a fresh dose of caffeine, then you already understand the importance of SEL. However important its topic, a meeting is unlikely to succeed if its participants feel disconnected. Similarly, if we want our children to succeed, we must do more than teach them academic skills in isolation. As educators, researchers, and scientists such as Mary Helen Immordino-Yang teach us about the importance of emotion and cognition to adolescent learning, SEL gains even more relevance. [5]

In the classroom, a teacher trained in SEL instructs first graders in reading with specific goals in mind: for the kids to be engaged in a book, to participate with each other in understanding it, and to think about how the ideas in the book connect to their lives. With an SEL framework, "reading" means more than decoding words on a page. Consider how much more engaging meetings will be when these first graders take their turn at the whiteboard!

Good teachers always have known that the learning process is both social and emotional—and less science than alchemy. A child's personality and life experience factor into every aspect of performance. In fact, nineteenth-century education pioneer John Dewey championed a Whole Child approach to education. Yet today, SEL is controversial. To some education policy experts, it's a clear path to student success. Others have termed it "lunacy." SEL opponents portray it as a distraction from a singular focus on academics, a separate and superfluous learning track. "You can't teach grit!" is their battle cry.

---

[4] "Education for Work and Life: Guide for Practitioners," National Research Council of the National Academies, http://sites.nationalacademies.org/cs/groups/dbassesite/documents/web page/dbasse_084153.pdf.

[5] Mary Helen Immordino-Yang and Antonio Damasio, "We Feel, Therefore We Learn: The Relevance of Affective and Social Neuroscience to Education," Mind, Brain, and Education, Blackwell Publishing, March 12, 2007, http://onlinelibrary.wiley.com/doi/10.1111/j.1751-228X.2007.00004.x/full.

But in practice, SEL always lives in conversation with other aspects of learning. Its supporters propose a "both/and" approach, not an "either/or" ultimatum.

The simplest (and worst) way to approach education policy is to make it black and white: my way good; your way bad. Ironically, this is exactly what SEL teaches kids to overcome: the need to dominate a discussion instead of listening and learning. In today's complex, fast-moving world, emotional resilience and empathy are essential. In fact, we need SEL in the corridors of power as much as in the corridors of our public schools.

To advocates who object to SEL on the grounds that it stigmatizes low-income children as being especially deficient in these skills, I would argue that if SEL isn't available in affluent public schools and private academies, then the children who attend them are seriously deprived. First, all our children would benefit from higher levels of resilience and empathy. The tragic "suicide clusters" that rocked the high schools of the well-to-do in Palo Alto just a few years ago show the urgency of that need.

Second, even if you view education solely through the pragmatic lens of preparing children for successful careers, SEL and Whole Child thinking unlock the key to the high-paying jobs of the twenty-first century. While many twentieth-century business functions can be performed well in relative isolation, digital technology requires an array of skills that no traditional K-12 curriculum offers. In his recent essay about gender and tech jobs,[6] former Google Distinguished Engineer Yonatan Zunger explains popular misconceptions about the hierarchy of engineering positions in a company like Google: "People who haven't done engineering, or people who have done just the basics, sometimes think that what engineering looks like is sitting at your computer and hyper-optimizing an inner loop [...]: something straightforward and bounded which can be done right or wrong, and where you can hone your basic skills."

---

[6] Yonatan Zunger, "So, about this Googler's manifesto," August 5, 2018, https://medium.com/@yonatanzunger/so-about-this-googlers-manifesto-1e3773ed1788.

He goes on to explain that while such tasks are common at the novice stages of engineering, the real work of engineering, the work of the successful professional, is both intuitive and interactive:

> "Engineering is not the art of building devices; it's the art of fixing problems. Devices are a means, not an end. Fixing problems means first understanding them—and since the whole purpose of the things we do is to fix problems in the outside world, problems involving people, that means that understanding people, and the ways in which they will interact with your system, is fundamental to every step of building a system."

And after you've grasped how people will interact with a system, do you go hide in a cubicle to write code? No. Instead you "quickly find that the large bulk of your job is about coordinating and cooperating with other groups." So, which skills define the successful senior engineer in Silicon Valley? "Essentially, engineering is all about cooperation, collaboration, and empathy for both your colleagues and your customers."

Zunger observes that he arrived at Google profoundly deficient in these skills: "It's a skillset that I did not start out with, and have had to learn through years upon years of grueling work." What if he'd gone to a school with SEL and a Whole Child approach? Without it, we simply aren't preparing any of our students, regardless of race or socioeconomic position, for optimum success in work or in life.

The Whole Child in History

Given how Whole Child and SEL are disparaged by some education "experts," you'd think they were newfangled trends, invented by hippies or imported from a socialist country. In fact, America's public school system was established by Whole Child–style reformers who called themselves the Progressive Education Movement. Back in the 1880s, Progressive Education stood in opposition to the typical nineteenth-century curriculum, which was based on the European model and aimed at preparing wealthy young men for university.

The Progressives opposed both the rote memorization favored in schools at the time and the idea that schooling was mostly reserved for the upper class. For John Dewey, a leading philosopher and reformer of the era, democracy was the highest ethical ideal, and education for all children regardless of background was essential to a democratic way of life.

Dewey championed what we today would call social and emotional learning. "I believe," he wrote in his famous Pedagogical Creed, "that all education proceeds by the participation of the individual in the social consciousness of the [human] race." School, Dewey asserted, is primarily a social institution, a "form of community life."[7] Education, he said, "is a process of living and not a preparation for future living."[8]

Dewey believed the process of learning had two components: social and emotional. "The child's own instincts and powers furnish the material and give the starting point for all education," he wrote, and the correct role of the teacher is to connect to an activity that the child has initiated independently. Anything else is merely "pressure from without." What would Dewey have thought about teaching to the test, the ultimate form of education as outside pressure? To him, the evils of the traditional European education system included "deadness and dullness, formalism and routine."[9] Sound familiar?

Progressives like Dewey believed that education meant getting your hands dirty, in cooking, sewing, and gardening for all children. They saw the development of social skills as core and were early promoters of collaborative and cooperative approaches to learning and projects that served the community. Instead of testing, they favored measuring a child's progress by evaluating his or her unique talents and activities. Teachers, they believed, should honor each child as an individual, behaving as mentors, with care and compassion.

This historical commitment to Whole Child education goes far beyond the United States. About ten years after Dewey published his

---

[7] John Dewey, "My Pedagogical Creed," School Journal, Vol. 54, January 1897, pp. 77-80, http://dewey.pragmatism.org/creed.htm.

[8] Ibid.

[9] Ibid.

Pedagogical Creed, the Italian educator Maria Montessori opened her first *Casa dei Bambini* (Children's House) in a working-class district in Rome, laying the foundation for the system of education practiced around the world today in Montessori schools.

Like in Progressive education, the Montessori method is grounded in an aversion to controlling the child from above. Instead, Montessori believed that when children are given freedom, they gravitate toward activities that connect deeply to their talents and aptitudes in developmentally appropriate ways, and develop an organic self-discipline that eliminates the need for punitive practices.

Care of the environment and the self were central themes in Montessori's classrooms. So was treating children as individuals, each with unique gifts and potential. Over time, Montessori began to see independence as the ultimate goal of education, defying the traditional European focus on conformity and discipline. Ironically, early twentieth-century Progressive educators considered her methods too rigid and inhospitable to imagination and play. By the time she was rediscovered in the United States in the 1960s, of course, American education had made a decisive pivot away from nurturing play and imagination.

Those of us who remember drama, music, and art class as minor yet meaningful parts of our own public school curriculum can thank the Progressives. They believed such activities aren't optional or ancillary, but central to education. I agree. The aptitude of children, Dewey wrote, should be aligned with the forces that elevate the human race, and children should perform "those fundamental types of activity which make civilization what it is."[10]

Because the Whole Child approach was present at the very establishment of public education in America, what the heck happened? Why is our system beset with high-stakes testing, the neglect of creativity, unhealthy competition, rigid perceptions of success and failure, and a fatally narrow view of what a child needs to learn to prepare her for the future?

An intriguing answer to this question is offered by my good friend, the renowned educator Elliot Washor. Elliot's nonprofit, Big

---

[10] Ibid.

Picture Learning, has established schools all over the country that put students at the center of their own education by working collaboratively, spending time on projects in their communities, and being guided by caring mentors who encourage them to develop the mind, hand, and heart.

Elliot recently visited Finland, which back in the nineteenth century adopted an education movement called "Sloyd." Sloyd taught woodcarving to all schoolchildren, not as vocational training, but to connect the hand, heart, and mind and to illuminate the mental journey from the tangible to the abstract by moving from woodwork to words. In the twenty-first century, Finnish schoolchildren are still using their hands at school, making objects from wood, ceramics, or metal. But when Elliot brought up the Sloyd movement, Finnish educators looked at him quizzically. No one had heard of it. The system had kept the practice but lost the philosophy behind it.

What caused our similar, if more alarming, scenario here at home? Not only have we lost the philosophy behind Progressive education, but we're losing the practice as well, with schools sacrificing the very classes that make children excited to learn: "Don't cut band, Superintendent!" the kids in Sacramento once implored me. "It's my reason for coming to school."

According to Elliot, the Progressive approach was first interrupted during World War I. Modern warfare operates through standardization and mechanization, and when America entered the war, our culture shifted toward celebrating and emulating those values. Tension arose between Progressive education and the traditional European model, which — much like a modern army — favored routine, discipline, and conformity. Eventually, this led to the Eight-Year Study, a 1933 project of the Bureau of Educational Research that analyzed student performance in schools across the country, aiming to settle the debate once and for all.

The study yielded a victory for Progressive education, which was objectively proven to generate better educational outcomes for children. And maybe at a different time, America's public schools would have made a decisive break with deadness, dullness, formalism, and routine. But soon World War II erupted, and the United States entered it. In a familiar cultural shift, the men who promoted classifying our soldiers through psychological testing, matching head circumference with managerial traits, and elevating IQ tests over human interactions won the day. Another wave of mechanization and standardization swept through our national institutions.

As these methods took over the field of education, the well-being of the child was left in the dust. Scientific data aimed at measuring narrow bands of competence became the gold standard in evaluating our children, while care and compassion were chased out of the classroom.

Just as our school system became racially integrated and society began to expect girls to become educated on the same range of topics and activities as boys, we gave up on the tools and approaches that had democratized education to begin with, changing it from an elite and rigid system to one that could serve all children by viewing each one as worthy and unique. In other words, we surrendered Whole Child values just when we needed them most.

"Science practiced badly produces standardization," says Elliot, "and you can't drive equity through standardization."

As we mobilize our education system to meet the needs of our children and the demands of twenty-first-century professions, we're standing on the shoulders of giants like John Dewey, whose vision encompassed the very challenge we face today. Modern technology changes so quickly that specific technical skills are far less relevant than analytical thinking and emotional intelligence. More than one hundred years ago, Dewey addressed this:

> "With the advent of democracy and modern industrial conditions, it is impossible to foretell definitely just what civilization will be twenty years from now. Hence it is impossible to prepare the child for any precise set of conditions. To prepare him for the future life means to give him command of himself; it means so to train him that he will have the full and ready use of all his capacities; that his eye and ear and hand may be tools ready to command, that his judgment may be capable of grasping the conditions under which it has to work. . . ." [11]

---

[11] Ibid.

Chapter 3

The Whole Child in Sacramento

The Whole Child and My First One Hundred Days

I mentioned my "corn dogs" moment in chapter two, when my children alerted me that education is as much about what we serve in the cafeteria as what we write on the whiteboard. Like so much of what I learned as a superintendent, my commitment to educating and developing the Whole Child came from kids: my own, and the 47,000 I served.

During my first one hundred days, I took a trip to John Morse (later Alice Birney), a Waldorf-inspired K-8 public school in southern Sacramento. I was visiting three schools a day at the time, and staying on schedule required limiting each visit to forty-five minutes. When I arrived at John Morse, something felt, looked, sounded, and even smelled very different than any other school I'd visited. I saw children's mud boots outside of classrooms. I saw gardens, natural plantings, and wood play structures everywhere. I heard singing, music, and laughter. I was greeted with genuine warmth and felt a sense of mutual respect among the children and adults.

I ended up staying two hours and visiting every classroom. In each one, children and adults were engaged in learning, sharing, and leading. My trip to John Morse stuck with me forever. What I saw that day was that when children, teachers, and parents are happy, the children thrive. It's about relationships. And the relationships on all sides of this diamond — what I like to call "The Magnificent Diamond" of child, teacher, family, and community — are at the very heart of Whole Child education.

The Whole Child Means Nutrition

Early in my tenure, during a visit to a second-grade classroom, a student named Anton approached me and asked, "Superintendent, why do we use Styrofoam trays in our lunch room that take fifty years to break down in a landfill? My classmates and I bring plates and utensils from home and wash them. Can't you to do something about it?"

Four months later, biodegradable trays were introduced into our lunch rooms and Anton and his family got the very first one, signed by the trustees of our school board. I loved how Anton applied what he'd learned in class to the real-life situation of his lunch room. How and what our students ate was always on my mind, because healthy children are better learners.

Thanks to a US Department of Agriculture grant, we were able to start serving fresh, locally grown strawberries to elementary school children at lunch. Nutritious food is essential to good health. Fresh strawberries were especially important to the kids whose parents couldn't afford to provide their lunches and relied on our lunch program every day.

We didn't stop there. To keep the momentum going, we launched a Healthy Food Task Force, which brought more nutritious, locally grown food to our schools.

Soon enough, fresh salad bars and local dairy, fruits, and vegetables became the norm in every elementary and middle school. I'll always remember watching second-grade students at Earl Warren Elementary

School (one of over a dozen schools in our district with 100 percent of children living at or below the federal poverty line and qualifying for free or reduced-priced lunch) helping themselves to fresh grapes, broccoli, and olives under the watchful eye of fifth graders ready to assist.

Our district had a responsibility to teach our students about food, nutrition, and the environment so they could advocate for the health of their own communities and be prepared for careers in healthcare, science, and the growing opportunities connected to alternative energy. As part of a local bond measure passed in the fall of 2012 to revitalize our schools, we included a plan for a central kitchen where we could prepare food for our children from locally grown and sourced fruits, vegetables, meats, and dairy products.

The Whole Child Means Music

> "Music has helped my time-management skills by having me make time for practice. In music, you must be organized and be responsible. My memorization skills have improved since I started playing an instrument. None of my other classes are like this. Music stays with you your whole life. It makes a happy environment where students are brought together by a common cause. Music brings unity."

This student testimonial says it better than a binder full of studies, but the studies are there, too. Arts education is not a frivolous add-on to a school curriculum. Years of research show that the arts are closely linked to almost everything we want for our children: academic achievement, character-building, civic engagement, and equal opportunity.

Scientists have detected growth in the parts of the brain tied to language and executive function in children who study music when they're young, and many believe that, at any age, musical training improves cognition. My students observed that music class supported their math skills.

"When I look at music notes, I don't seem confused," said one seventh grader. "I understand what is a whole note or quarter note, even half and eighth notes." Another student remarked, "If I put a math equation into fingerings or rhythm, I can remember it better."

Students also reported that music taught them discipline, perseverance, relationship skills, and responsible decision-making, and got them excited about learning: "Music helped me to be a better student because I persevered to play my instrument. At first, I thought I wasn't going to make it through and I was getting frustrated. But I pushed myself to keep going and I made it."

I was passionate about my district's participation in the Carnegie Hall LinkUP! for Music Education program, which brought music education—and professional musicians from the Sacramento Philharmonic—to more than 2,200 third through sixth graders from the region. Through partnerships with local ballet and opera companies, and by converting one of our schools to a performing arts studio (E. Claire Raley Studios), we managed to maintain and even increase arts programs in our schools despite drastic annual budget cuts, firm in my belief that an investment in the arts is an investment in society's future.

The passion for music went both ways. I remember two students—one from the projects and the other essentially homeless, traveling between extended-stay hotels with his mother—who started band in the seventh grade and made it into advanced band the following year. Despite housing and transportation barriers that would have thwarted many an adult, the two went on to represent their school at a local annual music festival. In just one year they became unstoppable, their love of music triggering a level of emotional growth and maturity their teachers found amazing.

In our shifting, unstable job market, the well-rounded, inspired, imaginative student will be better equipped for whatever awaits her. The ability to communicate, work in a team, and think outside the box are all recognized as skills crucial to success in twenty-first-century jobs. Our students, no less than any others, deserved a path into the "creative class"—where they were rewarded for creativity and collaboration, not rote tasks performed in repeat mode.

The Whole Child Means the Whole Year

At the time, prevailing attitudes in cash-strapped California were turn off the lights and the AC systems, and keep our schools open as few days as possible. The effect of this scarcity mentality was to deny our students critical forms of enrichment and learning, exposing them to what's referred to as "summer learning loss."

Children like mine had opportunities to attend summer camps or visit family in different parts of the country. But for many of Sacramento's children, closed schools meant more time at home watching television or on the streets in neighborhoods that couldn't offer structured learning opportunities or mentoring by older students and adults.

Enter Summer of Service, which invited first-year middle school and high school students to spend five weeks on their new campuses making new friends, meeting teachers, getting familiar with their new schools, and working on a community service project of their design under the watchful eyes of upperclassmen. Consider the multiple wins: kids comfortable in their new schools long before September, schools building culture and community, and adults and kids really getting to know one another and giving each ownership and voice.

I still vividly remember driving by McClatchy High School the Monday morning of the first day of summer vacation and seeing hundreds of students lined up waiting to get into school at 7:30 a.m.! Do kids vote with their feet? You bet. Why isn't Summer of Service replicated in schools across the country? Every parent, educator, and public servant should be asking that question.

The Whole Child Means Inclusion

Teaching with a Whole Child mindset means getting to know every child because every child is unique and learns differently. If my own children were the same age and sitting in the same classroom, they wouldn't thrive if they were taught the same way. How they learn and what interests them are different. With few exceptions, our public

education system does a poor job normalizing learning differently. We
have words like "differentiated instruction," and now "personalized
learning." But how can we really make learning differently normal?

Let's examine our approach to special education, which serves children with learning disabilities. For most children, special education
is a destination. Once they receive their "Individual Education Plan
(IEP)," they are entitled to receive services and supports largely funded by federal dollars. It's likely they will keep the "learning disabled"
designation throughout their K-12 education life. Here's the problem:
special education was never intended as a destination, but rather as
a series of supports and services aimed at reintegrating them into the
classroom. Yet today, most special-education services are delivered
via the so-called "pullout model," i.e., delivering instruction outside
of the regular classroom. What does it do to a child's sense of self to
be removed from his or her classroom and made to feel different?
With few exceptions, IEPs do not have to be delivered outside of
a classroom. Worse still are the isolated classrooms filled with children on IEPs. In California, these are called "special day classes." The
majority of children in these classrooms, stigmatized and separated
from their peers, are boys of color.

On my first day of school as superintendent in Sacramento, I took a
bus to an elementary school. As I walked through the campus greeting
parents and staff, one parent approached and asked me to go visit
Classroom 11. Finding a special day class for children with autism, I
asked the teacher if these kids ever had a chance to engage with other
children in the school.

"Oh no," she replied. "My children couldn't handle that."

But when and how would her children ever learn to engage, get along,
and build relationships with their peers? And what of the children outside Classroom 11? How will we teach them empathy and compassion?

There's one fact I've learned after visiting hundreds of classrooms
and schools: children learn from adults. When we model and have
mindsets that *reinforce* difference, we create environments for children
where being different isn't normal.

Instead of stigmatizing students who don't thrive with a traditional
curriculum, we should be developing unique learning profiles for all

our children, allowing us to really know who they are and teach them accordingly. We should emulate those schools that bring great intention and focus to climate and culture, applying social and emotional learning to behavioral issues and thus educating both mind and heart.

As one former public school principal who witnessed the effects of inclusive classrooms first-hand told me, "During our first year of full inclusion, we saw the number of special ed students performing at grade level in English language arts double. Behavior and anecdotal data, including parent feedback, indicated that students felt more connected to their peers and to the school."

By getting to know our children—how they like to learn, what they like to learn, when and where they like to learn—we would activate and engage them in their learning journey. More importantly, we would send them the very important signal that being unique and learning differently is normal. That's what educating and developing the Whole Child requires.

On the Beach

"How many of you boys have never seen the ocean before?" asked our drill instructor. A dozen young men assembled on a beach in Coronado warily raised their hands. "How many of you can't swim?" Another seven or eight raised their hands. "Don't worry," our instructor said, "I am trained to save you."

Hearing these reassuring words, forty teens from my district's Men's Leadership Academy program and a few adult chaperones, fully clothed and locked arm in arm, marched into the pounding, fifty-nine-degree Pacific surf. We were at the Naval Special Warfare Training Center near San Diego for a morning of team-building and physical fitness challenges with the elite Navy SEALs.

The Men's Leadership Academy sent talented, caring male mentors, such as instructor Malcolm Floyd, into district high schools and middle schools to teach leadership and life skills to at-risk young men. We knew the culture and climate of our schools mattered big time, and what better place to start than to cultivate these young men as "leaders" in their respective schools, neighborhoods, and communities? The program made them feel respected, listened to, cared for, and loved. It was one of several district initiatives aimed at empowering young people to take responsibility for their futures, programs that were contributing to the recent rise in Sacramento's graduation rates.

But rising rates are just numbers. I needed to see first-hand what effect the Academy was having. Spring break can be difficult for children from low-income urban neighborhoods. Most families lack the time and money to take a vacation, and many of the boys had never been outside of Sacramento, let alone 400 miles south to San Diego. How would these young men, brought together from five different Sacramento high schools, interact with each other? How would they carry themselves and respond to the stress and excitement of this strange new experience? What impression would we make on our hosts?

I was especially interested in the Academy as an antidote to our system's so-called "special education" policies, which tend to have a destructive and disproportionate effect on boys of color. Too often, these youngsters—targets of stereotypes and flawed assumptions— are isolated in programs that may make life easier for school administrators but abandon the children on a dead-end street. Initial data from the Academy showed improvement in grades, attendance, graduation rates, and, perhaps most importantly, attitude. But again, data is data. I needed to see for myself.

A day in the life of a Navy SEAL taught all of us what it's like to be pushed physically and mentally to levels higher than many of us had ever imagined. We learned about overcoming fear. We learned the importance of goal setting, visualization, positive talk, and strategies to deal with stress. We learned to work together and depend on each other— traits important for future success in school, work, family, and life.

After a morning spent carrying logs in team relay races, running and rolling in the giant sand berms, and marching into the cold Pacific, we tried to wash off sand and salt while the boys flashed tired smiles and shouted words of encouragement. We laughed! We screamed! These students, who had boarded the bus as kids from five different high schools in five different neighborhoods, were transformed into a cohesive team: one community of young men. I could see in their interactions that they'd experienced being part of something larger than themselves.

These young men knew as never before that the guys to their left and right had something in common with them, no matter what neighborhood or school they came from. In their comments and demeanor, they displayed the understanding that whatever their past or current circumstances, there was a future they could control and there were adults who believed in them, who saw their unlimited potential.

It's hard to convey how proud I was of our young men. The strong, favorable impressions they made on the Navy SEALs on Coronado reminded all of us just how special our children are, with incredible gifts and potential to match. The afterglow persisted for days after the trip, the sand in my hair reminding me how capable our young people are of growth and transformation, and how much we can accomplish when we reach the Whole Child—head, heart, and hands.

The Whole Child Means Family and the Power of Relationships

It goes without saying that parental and family involvement matters greatly in K-12 education. Thus, building trust among students, educators, parents, and families was fundamental and powerfully important. A school district like ours was required to think creatively and with great empathy when brainstorming ways to engage and empower our parents and families. Our efforts were grounded in a deep understanding about the fundamental importance of building trusting relationships between students and educators, and between educators and students' families.

Will a foreign-language speaker feel welcome at a parent-teacher conference? From Hmong to Spanish, parents in our district spoke dozens of languages at home. How does a formerly incarcerated parent experience entering a state-run institution like her child's school? Building trust, making parents feel welcome and wanted, and finding ways for them to support their child's learning was a top priority for me, especially as I recalled how my mother applied her own personal wisdom to my challenges when I was in the sixth grade. We needed to meet our parents and families where they were and on their terms, shifting the balance of power in favor of our families and children.

The enormous task of preparing our students for college and twenty-first-century careers—of making them agile thinkers and eager lifelong learners—was only made easier when we partnered with families to support their children's schooling. In the fall, the district's *Sacramento Goes Back to School* campaign encouraged every school principal to create a welcoming campus, opening the door to family involvement.

We followed up with a range of well-attended engagement events, from family math and science nights to fall carnivals and achievement celebrations after students took the California Standards Test. At every turn, we sought to establish a trusting dynamic and help parents recognize the importance of their involvement.

Thanks to a grant from Target, the district added Parent Resource Centers to select school campuses, where families could connect with programs and organizations aimed at helping them support their children's learning. The grant also helped fund Family Leadership Academies, workshops, classes, and courses focused on helping children succeed at school. We took that spark from our philanthropic partners to a new level by extending Parent Resource Centers into every single one of our schools, and used the Luther Burbank School's successful Parent University as a model to further empower our families. We needed our most important partners, our parents and families, to feel welcome in our schools.

Our next step was to introduce community reviews. At the heart of the Community School Review was an evaluation process created and run by parents and community members. Parents and students defined what school climate and culture should look like, then took turns in teams performing a qualitative review of their schools. You can imagine that many of our principals were initially uncomfortable with this idea. That was the point. Creating a culture of continuous improvement required feedback loops from our families, students, and community. It wasn't accountability in the "gotcha!" sense, it was accountability to get it right.

Yet even under the best of circumstances, not every student's parent will be able or willing to attend a school-based program. Some work too many hours, some are intimidated, some never had parents involved in their schooling, and some never went to school.

What are the hopes and dreams for your child? In Sacramento, we actively sought family engagement. Committed to building the level of trust required for a truly supportive school culture, we recruited our teachers into an innovative program called the Parent Teacher Home Visit Project (PTHVP), which trained district teachers and school staff on how to engage families in their children's education through visiting their homes. These words, asked by teachers on every first-time visit with a student's family, are at the heart of what makes this effort so vital and successful. In essence, it is the building block of creating trusting relationships among students, teachers, and families.

PTHVP, which the US Department of Education recognizes as a "high-impact" family engagement strategy, has been shown to improve attendance and test scores, reduce disciplinary actions, and decrease school vandalism. The program originated in Sacramento about ten years before my arrival, and I was overjoyed when, during my tenure, it was named one of the "Bright Ideas" by the John F. Kennedy School of Government at Harvard University for its low cost and collaborative structure.

A unique partnership among the school district, the local teachers' union, and a faith-based organization, the PTHVP worked because it nurtured trust, which is a rare commodity between people and state institutions. While home visits are used in a range of ways, they're usually associated with a negative event: a home assessment in response to a reported problem, a truancy investigation, or a social services intervention for a troubled family.

PTHVP is different: committed to family empowerment, it's an appointment between two willing participants—parent and teacher—not a "home invasion" by the state. In a Fox News report on a PTHVP program in St. Louis, the father of six-year-old Unafay observes: "She knows how much the teachers care when she sees them at her home." Parents, in turn, start coming to school events once they've witnessed first-hand the school's commitment to their family. Time and again, I heard principals and teachers cite a home visit as a turning point in creating an active partnership.

The positive outcomes of PTHVP inspired our academic parent-teacher teams. Anyone with school-aged children has experienced the traditional "drive-by" parent-teacher conference: in elementary school, you have twenty minutes with your child's teacher twice a year; in middle school, it's fourteen minutes with four teachers; and in high school, even if your child is struggling academically or socially, you're lucky to get one meeting a year, and then it's only fifteen minutes.

How much can we really expect to accomplish with this structure? What relationships can we expect to develop? Are we engaging our parents and families? Are we empowering our families and parents? These were the questions we asked, and the answer was clearly "No!"

What if we rethought this dynamic? What if we built off the success of our parent-teacher home visit program and the relationships it nurtured? We decided that instead of the traditional conferences, we'd invite families to come to class as a group. We'd show them data on their child's progress in math and English language arts, provide them with exercises they could do with their child at home to support their learning, and set some goals for the next class meeting in six to eight weeks.

Imagine classrooms full of parents (including several dads) co-taught by teachers who had the time to engage meaningfully with their children's parents and family members. It's a powerful example of how behavior and outcomes change when you alter the structure. And it all starts with a powerful question that both recognizes educators don't have all the answers and sends the signal we are here to listen. Imagine if we started every visit with families and communities by asking this simple question: *What are your hopes and dreams for your child?*

Our partnership with parents was also realized through adult education programs offered at our schools, featuring critical services such as career and technical training, English language classes, and courses that taught English learners how to help their children succeed in school. We put schools at the center of our neighborhoods, literally opening them up to give residents weekend access to school libraries, computer facilities, and, in some instances, the only green spaces in the area.

The notion of "community schools" became a reality, all the way to enlisting our families' support in keeping an eye on school security during vacation periods. It's pretty simple: when parents thrive, their children thrive. My passion to reach every child in my district meant doing everything possible to enrich the entire community.

Chapter 4

The Battle of the Budget

The Budget of 2010–2011

As 2009 drew to a close, I was expecting a budget shortfall of $18 million for the coming year. Then, on January 12, 2010, I learned that the state budget proposed by Governor Jerry Brown required us to cut more than $30 million from a $400 million budget.

In sharing the news with my district's 5,400 employees, I found myself quoting Buddhist monk Thich Nhat Hanh, who had worked to rebuild his ravaged country of Vietnam: "Hope is important because it can make the present moment less difficult to bear." Between California's fiscal crises, the volatile and unstable school funding system, and the effect of more than $144 million in cuts during the past six years, it was tempting to fall into despair.

To the greatest extent possible, my budget recommendations to the board of education were guided by the voices of the community. Faced with more than $30 million in reductions, we held forums to inform and educate our families about our fiscal challenges and to seek suggestions. I also met with a group of student-body representatives and asked them point blank: *If you were in my shoes, what would you cut, and what would be off the table?* One theme in particular resounded: "Don't cut band!" "It's my reason for coming to school." "It's my passion!"

We didn't cut band. In fact, driven by my passion to educate the Whole Child, I worked hard to add back more arts and music programs. Yet the voices of the community also were muted by the harsh realities of an underfunded system. In forums and surveys, class size arose as a core issue for parents and teachers alike. Studies are mixed on the effect of class size on learning, yet states spend millions to maintain or shrink their student-teacher ratios, and even if it's more intuition than science, no one wants overcrowded classrooms.

Early in the process, however, I was forced to deliver the sad news: increasing class size was just one of the options we had to consider, along with laying off 340 teachers; sixty counselors, social workers, and psychologists; and more than one hundred administrators. Adult education, school libraries, and student counseling were just some of the programs facing reductions or elimination.

Negotiations with the unions representing teachers and school staff were intense and emotional. Absent concessions affecting their work conditions and compensation, the district would risk fiscal insolvency and state takeover, forcing us to consider closing entire schools. Meanwhile, a critical deadline loomed: If, by March 15, a state-imposed deadline, the district failed to present a balanced budget, the Sacramento County Office of Education would begin taking over the district and make whatever cuts it deemed necessary.

By the middle of February, I had trimmed nearly $6 million from the district's administrative budget, yet we were still nearly $25 million short. With more than 85 percent of our costs tied to salaries and benefits, it was back to the negotiating table with the unions.

We tried every way possible to not turn this painful process into a tug of war between deserving educators supporting their families and deserving families facing drastic reductions in school services. It wasn't anybody's fault—at least, not anybody who stood to lose as we pared down an already gutted education budget.

At the beginning of March, I was quoted in the local media on a possible takeover by the county: "We would lose the right to make decisions about our own schools," I said. "That will not happen on my watch." Required by law to issue layoff notices by March 15—regardless of how many we might rescind by the close of negotiations—I reluctantly sought the board of education's approval to send pink slips to more than 700 teachers and school personnel.

Besides negotiating with the unions, I continually monitored California's legislature for changes to the state budget and lobbied for adequate and stable education funding. Superintendents located in state capitals such as Sacramento are obligated to fight on behalf of their colleagues throughout the state. Building relationships with political leaders and their staff is invaluable.

Late in March, following agreements that included unpaid "furlough days" with the SEIU, the Teamsters, and other unions representing school workers, I was happy to announce the rescission of 170 layoff notices. But negotiations with the Sacramento City Teachers Association (SCTA) were still unresolved, and I could offer my colleagues no definitive numbers on how many more layoffs might be rescinded or which programs might still survive. At stake for the teachers were reductions to benefits such as pensions and health insurance, as well as what was euphemistically termed "per-teacher contributions," i.e., actual cuts to their earnings.

On May 11, I was forced to announce that kindergarten through third-grade classes would be increased by five students to a total of thirty children, and that eighteen counseling positions would be eliminated.

"It's difficult to imagine those counseling office doors being closed to children in need," I wrote to my colleagues. "We are now at risk of losing good education professionals to other districts as these teachers and counselors, dealing with the anxiety and uncertainty of receiving a pink slip, explore options elsewhere."

My new community continually amazed me. Even as the threat of severe measures mounted, some of my teachers and students formed teams and worked with the district on an innovative plan that kept a school for adult education open and saved a range of adult English language classes, high school equivalency courses, and job training workshops.

By May 17, concessions from four of five unions had allowed us to rescind 462 pink slips. The only outstanding negotiation was with the teachers' union, the SCTA. Unless we could make headway, 240 educators would be laid off at the end of the year. In public and in private, I continued to assert my willingness to roll up my sleeves and work with the SCTA on an agreement we could all accept.

Understandably, Sacramento teachers had lots of questions. Most importantly, if they agreed to the painful concessions on the table, would the recovered money be used to rescind pink slips and fund programs that served our students? My answer was an emphatic yes. I had no intention of forcing teachers to make sacrifices only to enrich my administration or take back the unpaid furlough days I'd agreed to take off along with district staff.

In late May, during an event hosted by the Hmong, Mien, Lao Community Action Network, I spoke of the prevailing sense that, during these tumultuous times, we were all hanging on to the edge of a mountain by our fingertips. So many of our great teachers, counselors, and office staff could feel the dirt and rocks crumbling under their fingernails while they swayed in the wind. In these times of desperation, I told the audience, it's hard to imagine what the top of the mountain looks like.

Finally, on June 10, I was able to announce that negotiations with the SCTA had yielded a tentative two-year agreement that would save jobs, preserve important programs, and build toward the district's future financial stability. As a result, we were able to rescind ninety-one pink slips for our teachers. We also could bring back many middle school and high school counseling positions.

Though the news was good, I still recognized the horrific uncertainty some of our best teachers and staff had experienced—and which they would continue to feel—as we worked out the details of our staffing model.

"The state budget crisis has left our district grotesquely underfunded," I wrote to my colleagues. "Every day has seemingly presented us with a new challenge that tests our unity and collective strength."

The Budget of 2011–2012 and Beyond

Perhaps most trying was that even as our immediate worries subsided, everyone knew that the next year was coming and would bring with it another round of wrenching dilemmas and enraging choices. Indeed, by January 2011, it was *déjà vu* all over again: another potential shortfall in the tens of millions, another threatened takeover, another battery of pink slips issued to talented educators who deserved much better.

Everything brought a fight. Repairing the crumbling infrastructure of schools built during the Eisenhower era would require Sacramento voters to pass a bond measure, which they'd refused to do for a dozen years. To forestall truly cruel cuts to our children's education, California voters would have to extend temporary taxes in a June 2011 special election.

"We must plan for the prospect that voters, wearied by the recession and wary of tax increases, may reject the [extension]," I warned my colleagues.

Even before the voters could decide, the Legislature had to vote for the tax extension to appear on the June ballot. As required by Prop 13, a two-thirds vote was needed, yet another uncertainty the school board had to weigh as it moved forward with its legally mandated budget balancing duties. On March 4, 2011, I wrote to my colleagues:

> At last Thursday's board of education meeting, some impressive scholar-athletes from Hiram W. Johnson High School spoke passionately about the life-changing role of campus athletics, hoping to save sports from severe budget cuts. Instead, these articulate students had to face the gut-wrenching reality of public school financing at a time of epic underfunding.
>
> Trustees made the painful decision to cut another $13.6 million from the 2011–12 budget—including the elimination of funding for sports, yearbook, drama, cheerleading, newspaper and speech and debate. These further cuts allow [us] to submit a balanced budget proposal to the [county] by its March 15

deadline, staving off a "negative" rating which would put the district on the road to a state takeover.

The cuts, in addition to $14.5 million in reductions approved by the board on February 17, account for a deficit of $28.1 million for next year, our "worst-case scenario." That's the dire situation we will find ourselves in unless current temporary taxes are extended by voters in a June special election. With the temporary taxes kept in place, our deficit would be about $9.2 million.

After months of exhausting grassroots efforts by the teachers, parents, and administrators of my district, both the local and state measures passed. And again, even as we celebrated our victory, I had to remind us all to brace ourselves—the next year would bring yet another round of battles, all in the name of giving the children of Sacramento a decent shot in life.

Again, nothing came without a fight. Over time, it was this dynamic that sapped hope and energy from my colleagues and me. Our work was the education of California's next generation and yet, every step of the way, our progress was blocked and our efforts were thwarted. What does this say about our priorities as parents, as adults, as a country?

Part of the answer lies in dramatically improved communication. That first spring, I'd started writing weekly "Dear Colleague" letters to all staff and sharing them with the community. It was my way of keeping everyone informed. We also introduced community budget forums, and I'll always remember when a staff member approached me after one of them. As the operator of our portable sound systems, he'd been with me at all seven community budget discussions.

"Superintendent," he said, "I know I might lose my job given how dire our situation is, but thank you for helping me finally understand why, and what's at stake for our children."

When superintendents face urgent fiscal challenges, authentic engagement with students, families, staff, partners, and community is essential. Stakeholders must be involved in tough decisions, both for input and to ensure they understand the process when difficult choices have to be made. That is the only child-centered approach, one that gives voice to the children themselves and to the community and caregivers who touch the lives of those children daily.

Is it too much to ask that we proceed collaboratively when making decisions about our children's education? It's not about politics; it's about values. Unless we put children first when we plan our budgets, our priorities as a society are focused elsewhere, not on our youth and the future of our country.

Chapter 5

Impoverished Schools Improved;
Superintendent Sued

Putting a Marker Down with Priority Schools

In the spring of 2010, the state of California published a list of its lowest-performing public schools. In our district, only Oak Ridge Elementary appeared among the bottom 5 percent, yet by our own internal review of data, we believed several more were equally underperforming. So, in the spring of my first year in California, we set a course aimed at forever changing some of the poorest schools and neighborhoods in Sacramento by establishing what we termed "Superintendent's Priority Schools."

The goal was as simple as it was radical: transform the experience of students in our lowest-ranked schools by prioritizing leadership, resources to build teacher knowledge and skills, and family engagement. The goal was to create campuses that defied complacency and reached for greatness.

The plan we submitted to the California Department of Education didn't propose closing underperforming schools or converting them into charter schools. Instead, we sought to transform them, deploying carefully selected principals and teachers with the skills and dedication to get the job done.

Of the six underperforming schools we targeted, only Oak Ridge Elementary appeared on the official bottom 5 percent statewide list, and because of this, our plan was rejected. The department of education wasn't interested in our proposal to change the lives of hundreds of students. Its underlying message was maddening: the schools weren't bad enough. Even though we knew that the need for change was desperate and urgent, to the department it was simply a compliance issue, with no children's names or faces attached.

What did we do? We proceeded with our own plan. Scavenging the district budget for discretionary dollars, we plowed forward with no state or federal department of education–mandated strings attached. The following year, when the California state superintendent came to Oak Ridge to announce state testing results, our "official" low performer had the highest growth in test scores, more than every other bottom 5 percent elementary school in the state!

While millions of federal dollars spent on school improvement grants across the country failed to move the needle at all, the Superintendent's Priority Schools program defied the odds, outperforming comparable schools in the state. After just two years, several of our Priority Schools earned the highest rating in the California Office to Reform Education (CORE) school quality index, qualifying them as models for other low-performing schools.

Combining both academic and nonacademic metrics, the CORE index was the strongest holistic accountability measure in the country. Academic metrics included test scores with absolute scores and growth scores, as well as graduation rates. Nonacademic measures looked at the culture and climate of schools, including indicators of student social and emotional health.

In a school system ravaged by the worst financial crisis in fifty years, we showed our community, the state, and the nation what our neediest children can do when the adults in charge commit to the right educational supports and high expectations. Despite all the changes we made, some as large as hiring new leadership and staff and some as small as deep cleaning and painting, there was one fact we didn't change at all: who the kids were!

Priority Schools: Going Behind the Curtain

As I reflect on the Priority Schools, I'm struck by how much they represent a microcosm of all the problems, solutions, and pitfalls involved in reinventing K-12 public education. We had it all: the good, the bad, and the ugly. It's the Priority Schools I think about when I take stock of our systemic challenges, when I inventory our most promising remedies, and when I ponder the unintended consequences we invite when attempting to problem-solve a situation that requires structural change.

Sacramento—and our low-performing schools in particular—faced the same thorny cluster of systemic issues as every impoverished school district, including scant and/or misdirected resources, low and biased expectations, demoralized and underperforming teachers, performance metrics based on high-stakes testing, outdated teaching methods, and lack of family and community engagement. Accordingly, our plan for the Priority Schools took a systemic approach, deploying Five Design Principles that reflected the educational best practices we believed would support transformation:

1. Strategic staffing and facilities improvement

2. Rigorous student work

3. Professional training and collaboration

4. Family and community engagement

5. Organizational transformation

These were bolstered by strategies we called our Four Key Areas:

1. The use of data

2. A focus on literacy (reading and writing)

3. Student and family engagement

4. Collaborative and common practices

What this list masks are the huge risks we took with this transformative effort. Facilities improvement is a no-brainer. Faculty, staff, and students alike undoubtedly feel better showing up in schools where the toilets flush and the paint isn't peeling. But consider rigorous student work. We weren't starting from scratch. Depending on which grade they were in, our Priority Schools students had been exposed to between one and eleven years of substandard pedagogy. On top of that, three of our Priority Schools were absorbing students from seven neighborhood schools the district had closed, adding to the stress and disorientation of all involved. Can students under such circumstances be expected to pivot with any degree of success?

Similarly, our Priority Schools teachers weren't in their first year on the job. In some cases, they weren't in their first decade! Yet here we were, requiring they teach their students to interpret, analyze, synthesize, and evaluate the information presented in their classrooms. This comment by one of our teachers underscores the risk of failure this posed to the kids and adults alike: "We've been pushing so long just to recall the information. Now we're asking them to do something completely different."[12]

Even a seemingly straightforward area like collaborative and common practices among educators became a barrier to overcome. As it turned out, our teachers and administrators had never been encouraged or enabled to operate collaboratively, to share what worked and didn't work in their own classrooms and schools, and to develop the camaraderie and teamwork that, in so many settings, can make a seemingly impossible challenge not just doable, but deeply rewarding.

Notably, our Priority Schools teachers responded enthusiastically to the new normal, reporting feeling pride in their schools, a willingness to take risks and innovate, and a sense of peer support that gave them the courage and energy to go elbow-deep into our transformative process. In particular, our teachers internalized the practice of using

[12] "Priority Schools Report," p. 18, The BERC Group, October 2013.

data to assess their students' performance and to create customized solutions for those children the data showed were falling behind. This allowed for what one teacher called "big-time intervention."

"It goes back to how we look at the data," another teacher commented. "We don't leave a single kid out."[13]

Of course, the good news is that despite the risk we took, the schools succeeded. Viewed by growth in the Academic Performance Index (API), the state of California's accountability metric, the Priority Schools outperformed both other Sacramento schools and schools throughout the state. API growth increased between 2010 and 2013, yet declined in the other schools over that same period.[14]

Similarly, the Priority Schools outperformed the others in raising English Arts Proficiency scores, and our only Priority high school, Hiram W. Johnson High, outperformed other high schools in AP, SAT, and ACT test participation rates. Normally, when the pool of students taking tests expands, scores go down to reflect the addition of less-qualified pupils. Yet our Priority high school bucked this trend, holding steady on SAT and ACT scores even as participation rates climbed.[15]

But here's where the results get interesting. According to a report issued by the renowned BERC Group, our Priority Schools' educators weren't very successful in shifting their teaching methods.[16] Considering the barriers they faced, that's to be expected. What's surprising is that student performance improved nonetheless. So, which of the Five Design Principles did our teachers and schools successfully deploy? The BERC Group's highest scores were in use of data and family communication and engagement.[17]

"We talk about student data," one teacher reported, "and work together in grade-level teams to analyze student work. We give feedback to students to work on their weaknesses."[18] This individualized

---

[13] Ibid., p. 23

[14] Ibid., p. 45

[15] Ibid., pp. 58–64

[16] Ibid., pp. 17, 19, 30

[17] Ibid., p. 11

[18] Ibid., p. 22

attention deepened the student-teacher relationship. Meanwhile, pro-active home visits, frequent phone calls, and in-school events forged bonds between teachers and families, positioning parents as active partners in their children's education. The school "really educated us on what is expected of us and the kids," one parent reported. Parents learned how to "build their [children's] self-esteem to keep them motivated and interested." [19]

One of the core principles of social and emotional learning is being open to a both/and approach instead of insisting on either/or. The success of the Priority Schools exemplifies the value of this framework. Looking at the BERC Group's numbers—while many factors were in play—it's clear the quantitative and qualitative com-bination of data and communication, accountability and warmth, and rigor and human bonds were the core foundations for improved student performance.

Amid all the good news, however, it's important to highlight the big-picture problem that our Priority Schools also represent. To mis-quote James Carville, "It's structural, stupid!" What happened when our Priority Schools set new standards for teachers? Predictably, all the best teachers in those schools rolled up their sleeves and got to work. Meanwhile, the lower-performing, less engaged teachers who happened to work in the newly designated Priority Schools decided it was time to go elsewhere. We call them unintended consequences. Of our seven Priority Schools, three were middle schools. What do you think happened to the other middle schools in our district? They became the repository of middle school teachers who weren't on board with innovation, who weren't curious, or excited, or motivated by lofty standards. Therefore, even as the Priority middle schools got better, some of their non-Priority counterparts declined.

Another deeply structural challenge is leadership succession. Since the BERC Group's assessment in 2013, the fates of the Priority Schools have varied greatly. Some continue to see rising performance while others have slumped. The slump is because of two issues familiar to anyone who works in public education: unreliable leadership and

---

[19] Ibid., p. 42

institutional inertia. We celebrate the highly talented and charismatic individuals who can turn around a failing school, but what happens when they leave?

Once again, it's structural. School districts shouldn't have to rely on the all-too-few exceptional leaders who come and go, leaving a record of success but a runway to nowhere. The problem must be addressed on both ends. First, we need effective leadership training for our administrators so that replacing a great principal doesn't lead to declines in performance.

Second, once innovative values and methodologies have proved successful in experimental settings such as the Priority Schools, they should be enshrined in the district's practices and processes and eventually shared with school districts and states. This is structural change, grounded in vision. Otherwise, we sacrifice sustainability and growth, as happened in Sacramento. The Priority Schools were meant to be replicated if they performed as planned. However, real scaling hasn't occurred. Imagine how many lives would be affected if the triumphs we witnessed daily in the Priority Schools were happening in every one of the district's classrooms — and beyond.

Battle with the Union

> "In the Sacramento City Unified School District, [Jonathan Raymond] got around teacher tenure by setting up 'priority schools' in Sacramento's poorest neighborhoods. He was promptly sued and hounded until the day he resigned, while his priority schools were constantly badmouthed by the local teachers union."
>
> —Marcos Breton, *The Sacramento Bee*, June 11, 2014

It's true: my Priority Schools plan did defy teacher tenure rules, and the union did sue me. For this, I will never apologize. Using seniority alone to rank the value of individual teachers — to decide who gets laid off and who stays — is a lousy way to serve our students. What sense does it make to retain a mediocre or burned out teacher with ten years under the belt while an effective, dynamic teacher with five years' experience gets a pink slip and moves to another state?

The Priority Schools got the benefit of the "best of the best" educators from our district. We assigned those who would excel at motivating, inspiring, and educating children who'd been trapped in crumbling buildings and overcrowded classrooms, who'd been given the message over and over that the system didn't care about their educations or their lives. Never underestimate the insight our kids possess! They know full well when the people in charge consider them disposable, and these children come to life when we surround them with love, attention, and expectations of excellence.

Against the backdrop of layoffs required by our dwindling budget, creating Priority Schools meant tangling with the teachers union, and shortly after the teaching assignments for the year were posted, my district was served. In the end, the suit came to nothing. The judge who ruled in our favor addressed head-on the impossible choices we faced in his decision:

> *"The district faced a difficult challenge in implementing budget cuts requiring the layoff of 400 employees while providing the best education possible for Sacramento's children. The district sought to navigate Scylla and Charybdis: Retaining teachers it believed necessary for its innovative Priority Schools, yet honoring the seniority rights of experienced teachers."*

The Priority Schools withstood the lawsuit, and our school board showed great courage in supporting them when in other school districts, such as San Francisco's, it did not. But the controversy surrounding Priority Schools did nothing for teacher morale. Instead of representing all the benefits that can happen when a community pulls together for its most vulnerable children, they became another reminder of how divided our educational system has become.

The Broad Academy did me no favors when it came to union relations. "People who come from outside education are more used to working in performance culture versus entitlement culture," Broad's director told *The Sacramento Bee* when my appointment was first announced. Disparaging hard-working educators by calling them "entitled" is not how I would have set the table.

Recent data have shown that compared to other professionals with similar credentials, teachers see a wage gap of 17 percent. For nonunion teachers, that gap jumps to 25.5 percent. Here the question of societal values arises. However problematic I find tenure rules, and however outrageous it is that poorly performing teachers are hard to discipline or dismiss, it's obvious why teachers cling to a union model that interferes with critically needed systemic change. Sadly, America has sent teachers a message that we value other professions more than we value theirs. This, too, is a structural issue confronting public education and our nation as a whole.

Leadership is about showing respect to the people whose lives you affect with your decisions, and its well past time for policy makers to be better leaders when it comes to education. All voters, especially parents, should demand that decisions about school funding occur in an environment that's data-driven, civil, respectful of all stakeholders, and—above all—free of ideology. The issue is not "performance" versus "entitlement," it's about using our resources to ensure that our children flourish. This can only happen when the adults working with our children are respected, supported, and prepared to perform in real-world classroom conditions with the diverse needs of our children.

In an ideal scenario, Sacramento's Priority Schools would not have placed the district between Scylla and Charybdis, the mythical monsters from Homer's *Odyssey*. The Priority Schools would not have sparked a lawsuit because every teacher who deserved a job would have had one. In an ideal scenario, mediocre teachers could readily access resources for improving and supporting their performance, including mentoring and coaching from master teachers and instructional leaders.

If we educated and developed the Whole Child, which also means educating and developing the whole adult, burnout wouldn't be an issue. Teachers would be prepared and supported for the challenges they face in schools and classrooms. They could teach instead of contending with the fallout of intractable poverty, untreated physical and mental illness, and the other burdens our underprivileged children bring to school. Teachers would feel hopeful, empowered, and supported rather than hopeless, powerless, and alone.

However, let's be clear: we don't need to aim for an "ideal scenario," that candy-coated situation that's always out of reach. Sacramento's Priority Schools, and similar efforts all over the country, demonstrate that when Whole Child education is implemented by caring, qualified educators—and such educators exist in large numbers—children thrive and excel. As you'll see in subsequent chapters, it's happening right now. It's not "ideal"; it's real.

Leaving Sacramento

After almost five years in Sacramento, we had much to be proud of. Since my arrival, we'd succeeded not only in establishing Priority Schools, but in replicating successful programs such as Waldorf-inspired public schools, creating early kindergarten programs and Hmong and Chinese language-immersion programs, growing International Baccalaureate programs, and expanding college and career pathways.

We'd started supporting our teachers to implement an inquiry-based approach to meet new math and English language standards. We'd created partnerships with our local community and four-year colleges, and brought social and emotional learning and a Whole Child approach to preparing children for college, careers, and life. We expanded off-site and summer learning, established a compact on working and learning with our charter school partners, made greening our schools a priority, passed two school bond measures to support these efforts, transformed how Sacramento's public school children were fed, and joined a few other California districts to receive the only school district waivers to No Child Left Behind.

Despite these accomplishments, in October 2013, I informed my colleagues that my last day as superintendent would be December 31, 2013. This also had been the year we closed several schools in Sacramento—a decision that seemed necessary given our massive deficit, but which pitted me against the people living in the affected neighborhoods and raised a storm of accusations and threats—not just against me, but against my family.

Shuttering schools is time-consuming, exhausting, and inevitably ugly. I certainly wasn't going to leave something like this to a successor. My advice to superintendents contemplating school closings is to always think twice: The promised cost savings may fail to outweigh the conflicts, bitterness, and the community's loss of faith in the system.

I had taken a month off that summer to recuperate from the bruising school closures during which my wife Julie asked me whether I was ready to leave Sacramento. My answer: I didn't know. Maybe it was time.

Could I have stayed until the summer of 2014 to finish the school year? Sure. I was tough and resilient. With the support of my family, friends, and a network of colleagues, I could have withstood the 24/7 intensity, the competing needs and pressures, the responsibility for so many lives. I could have stayed, measuring meaningful victories against a relentless tide of defeats. Not my defeats, but losses to the community, to the parents, children, and teachers of Sacramento, who all deserved better.

However, the prospect of staying on felt daunting. And when a job opportunity arose that would enable me to move my family back to Boston, I accepted with some reluctance. Yet in addition to my mounting sense that I needed a better way to affect public education, I realized that living so far from extended Boston-area relatives was difficult for my wife and children.

The day the moving truck pulled up to our Sacramento home, I was still boxing things up and throwing away what we wouldn't need. As I rushed around the house, something caught my eye. Thumbtacked to the wall by my desk was that infamous cartoon from *The Sacramento Bee*: me, in a fresh white apron, confronting the mess I'd been hired to clean up. I smiled wryly, reassured about my decision to move on. The chaos I'd been tasked with reining in had abated. The district was now running smoothly, its future in good hands thanks to the people we had brought in and empowered.

If I had to pick the single biggest reason I left, it was the children I'd fought for every day in Sacramento and those just like them in cities and towns across our nation. Something more had to be done. My overriding priority was to find a way to bring more light, to find another and better way. And so, after running as long and as hard as I could, I passed the baton and headed out on a new race.

Chapter 6

From Broad to Sacramento

After I shared an early draft of this book with some of my peers, I received a response that surprised me at first, then made me realize just how much I had changed as an educator and as a person since my graduation from the Broad Academy. Like a student in a really good school, my journey had given me an adult education in social and emotional learning!

It started like this: One of my readers took me to task for thinking the only problem in education is a "belief gap." He thought I was arguing that gaps in achievement and opportunity don't exist. This really made me scratch my head. While I clearly expressed my discomfort with the term "achievement gap," I thought I'd been clear about why.

Differences in outcomes do exist between white children and children of color. Under No Child Left Behind, the achievement gap became associated with high-stakes tests that, for many, exacerbated the very gaps the law was written to close.

It's true that I used a quote that identified our "belief gap" as the real issue in education. In a way, I agree. Words like "achievement gap" and "opportunity gap" ask us to view disadvantaged children only in relation to their more advantaged peers. Is that helpful? Or does it interfere with our ability to view each child as a precious, talented individual, and to believe all children can succeed, given the right tools and a caring, compassionate environment? *That belief must come first.* A truly effective school system will be guided by a powerful belief in all its children, not by an aspiration to raise test scores.

What really struck me about the feedback was that it lacked a "both/and" perspective. Yes, differences in opportunity and achievement exist, and if we don't start by believing in our children, those differences or variances or gaps—whatever call them—will remain. Then it occurred to me that both/and was not a perspective I had always applied myself. My both/and framework evolved over time, on my journey from freshly minted Broad Academy graduate to seasoned superintendent of a richly diverse urban district.

The Broad Academy tended to view "school reform" in a traditional, metrics-driven way. While Broad was essential to my success as an educator, parts of my evolution came later, from other sources. I would say those sources came in two categories: the mentors who influenced and shaped me, and the experiences I had and processed over time that forced me to think in more complex and elastic ways.

In my first job, as chief accountability officer of the Charlotte-Mecklenburg Schools, I was fortunate to work under Superintendent Peter Gorman. Pete is also a Broad graduate, and a man of integrity, intellect, and good humor. He was an excellent role model for honoring the education I got from Broad, while also keeping an open mind about new tools and frameworks.

Like my sixth-grade teacher Harry Boyadjian, Pete showed me patience and encouragement when I arrived in Charlotte. Instead of feeling like "the new guy," I was welcomed as part of his team and eagerly dove into my new responsibilities. My title carried a stigma of sorts. For some people, "accountability" means metrics-driven pressure, the worst manifestation of a standardized approach to education that discourages creative, thoughtful, individualized instruction. And while some accountability professionals do operate like that, I knew right away that I didn't want to be the new sheriff in town, brutally enforcing standards and punishing outliers.

Fortunately, Pete didn't want a sheriff. His belief about the role of accountability was best summed up when he said, "You can't just put hammers in your toolkit." There's no law saying that the use of data must be coupled with pressure and punishment. For Pete, data was a management tool that kept favoritism and subjective beliefs out of the evaluation process.

Instead of viewing students through a prism of bias or assumptions, data—when used correctly—can help identify where a teacher should apply extra effort and which topics could benefit from more effective instruction. Data itself is information. If it's used to judge, disparage, or punish students or teachers, then it's being abused.

This perspective would ultimately help me shape the agenda of the Priority Schools and negotiate with my Waldorf schools to achieve the right balance between independence and alignment with the district. In Charlotte, I focused on coupling the concept of accountability with the concept of support and pressure. The three should always go hand in hand: Once a problem is identified, true accountability means finding and offering supports to help solve it, and together, they create a positive pressure to drive toward continuous improvement.

In Charlotte, we believed an accountability officer should operate with clarity, context, and candor. What does this mean? Let's say our assessment shows that 50 percent of an elementary school's children are proficient in reading. Okay—now we have clarity on the data, but what's next? We need to surround our finding with context: Last time we tested, only 30 percent of children showed proficiency, which suggests a positive trend. Instead of coming down hard on the language arts teachers, how about working collaboratively to identify how they achieved the increase and revising the curriculum to emphasize those elements of success?

Where does candor fit in? Let's be honest with our teachers, our parents, and our district. Based on how long it took to raise scores twenty points, we can project forward. It's going to take another ten years before the school reaches 100 percent proficiency in reading. That candor is crucial. It takes undue pressure off teachers and administrators, who can't be expected to snap their fingers and get to 100 percent in a year. It sets realistic expectations and lays the groundwork for ongoing accountability.

Coming in as an outsider, my first instinct was to question whether "the way we've always done it" was the best way forward. I was lucky that Pete was my boss. Instead of stifling me, he encouraged me to keep tinkering with the balance between accountability, support, and pressure, and to hold on to a larger vision instead of letting the day-to-day drown it out.

When a school board member once chided me, saying "hope is not a strategy," Pete offered me a new way to think about the issue. It's both/and, he said. Hope may not be the strategy, but it has to be the first step in developing a strategy, and in creating the vision that's needed to mobilize change: "You have to believe it before you can see it." It was hope and belief that allowed me to think big in Sacramento and make good on my duty to "take risks for kids."

I brought a lot of my Charlotte experience with me to Sacramento, including a balanced view of the role of data and an understanding of where hope and belief fit into the work of a leader. On a practical level, I adapted the Charlotte model of strategic staffing for the Priority Schools, moving high-performing educators into low-performing schools and giving them the freedom and flexibility to apply creative solutions.

As the plan for the Superintendent's Priority Schools took shape in Sacramento, I had a moment that really showed me how far I'd come in my journey as an educator. Back in my Broad Academy days, two people I much admired were prominent urban superintendents: Rudy Crew of the Miami-Dade Public Schools and Manuel Rivera of the Rochester City School District. Rivera, who in 2006 was named Superintendent of the Year by the American Association of School Administrators, made significant improvements to language arts and math proficiency in Rochester even as he trimmed $30 million from the budget.

Crew, who earned Superintendent of the Year two years after Rivera, gained national prominence for his work in Miami, boosting its graduation rates and earning recognition from Newsweek, the

Kennedy School of Government, and Broad Academy, where he was a finalist for the Broad Prize three years running.

Here were two of the greatest minds in public education. As a Broad student, I saw myself as a dry sponge, ready to soak up the wisdom of these exceptional leaders. So, I mounted a campaign, asking each of them for an opportunity to shadow them on the job. I wouldn't take no for an answer and visited both. I ended up spending a week with Rudy in Miami, by his side during his fourteen-hour days. Little did I know I would one day succeed him as superintendent in Sacramento, a position he had held from 1988 to 1993!

Fast forward to Sacramento, and the beginning stages of the Priority Schools. As I wrestled with the California Department of Education and scrambled for alternative ways to fund the plan it had rejected, I got a visit from my friends Rudy and Manny. They had recently teamed up to form Global Partnership Schools, a consultancy focused on turning around low-performing schools. They offered to take the Priority Schools off my hands: "Give us your bottom 5 percent schools, and we'll raise student achievement."

It was tempting. With all my other challenges—constant battles over budgets, crumbling campuses, pink-slipped teachers, and pressure to scrap the programs that inspired kids the most—handing over my low-performing schools to recognized experts would have been a sensible move. But being sensible was not in the cards: I was driven by passion, my commitment to children, and love.

"You guys are going to think I'm crazy," I told them. "But I can't turn my kids over to someone else. If I learned one thing from the two of you, it's to stand up and lead when the chips are down. I may fail at this, but I'm the one who has to take the risk." At that moment, I felt I was a superintendent not just by title, but in my head, heart, and hands. My mentor Tom Payzant had told me being a superintendent means knowing what to do when you don't know what to do. And I knew, without a doubt, that the Priority Schools were my mission. This was a great milestone in my journey.

The truth about a learning journey like mine is that it never ends. Just recently, I had the chance to speak with a fantastic Sacramento principal, Eric Chapman. He had so impressed me during my tenure in Sacramento. His drive to serve his children in every way he could was relentless, from washing floors when custodians were cut to forging strong ties with local community leaders who acted as mentors to his students.

The conversation we had was difficult, but cathartic. We spoke of the current conditions at the Priority Schools. Sadly, many of our achievements had reversed course. Because of that enraging cycle where gains are rewarded by loss of funds, the Oakridge School had lost its improvement grant and its all-star teachers were leaving. As dedicated professionals, they saw their talents squandered. Instead of teaching, they were filling in for all the social workers, librarians, and other critical support staff who'd been cut.

Families were leaving too. Oakridge alone had lost one hundred families, who knew their kids were no longer safe and taken care of. Who can blame them? If there's no open dialogue with the district, no bond of trust, and no commitment to listen and care, their only option is to vote with their feet. It honestly made me feel like crying. I felt for everyone: the disappointed parents, the teachers whose dignity and professionalism were being sidetracked, and most of all the children whose futures were now at risk, and who were being deprived of the education, the warmth, and the community they deserved.

Part of me was filled with regret. "Eric," I said. "Should I have stayed?" It's a question that came up often. This wasn't the first time I'd heard about downward trends since my departure, of drop-offs in graduation rates, and of scores going down instead of up for disadvantaged Sacramento children. Eric's reply filled me with a sense of peace.

"Jonathan," he said, "you shined the light and showed us how to lead. You modeled a set of values. If we can't carry them forward, then shame on us. We have to own it. The work is never finished. Nobody can stay forever." The work is never finished. Nobody can stay forever. It's true. That's why I'm so emphatic about making the community a partner. One day, Eric will leave his school, too, and whatever his replacement brings, it won't be Eric's decades of experience with his teachers and staff, or his unique charisma and determination.

You know who won't leave? The community. A wise new leader will be guided by the families and local leaders who know what their children need. When I arrived in Sacramento, I knew intuitively that I had to spend my first one hundred days out in the community, even if I didn't know why. As a brand-new superintendent, I didn't yet understand that nobody stays forever, except for the community.

I didn't know that when I was offered the chance to offload my greatest challenge to a pair of trusted experts, I would decline. I didn't know I would appoint the country's first chief family and community engagement officer, or fight to preserve and expand arts programs in schools serving our most disadvantaged children. I didn't know that balancing accountability, support, and pressure would shape some of my biggest decisions, or that hope would lead me to stay for four-and-a-half years.

Looking back, I'm humbled and inspired to see that I myself was the student and that I gained in social and emotional learning along the way. Like Harry Boyadjian, my mentors didn't force-feed me facts and statistics; they saw me as a whole person, and they nurtured all of me: head, heart, and hands. I can't think of a stronger argument for Whole Child education. Every one of us needs it, and we have the opportunity to give it to our children, who hold our future in their hands.

Chapter 7

Deep Listening, Shared Vision, and Giving Students Voice

Leadership and Listening

My tenure in Sacramento was an incredibly rare opportunity, a time when I could have a positive effect on children's lives. School superintendents are given the power and authority to take steps that can very quickly make meaningful changes. When Anton, that courageous student, challenged me to get rid of Styrofoam lunch trays, I was in a position to act and within four months, the trays were gone. Superintendents have the power to make choices and the choices we make establish priorities upon which others, too, can act.

It all starts with listening.

Anton created a teachable moment for both of us: He got me thinking about the environmental effects of the materials our district was using, and—just as importantly—he and his classmates got to experience how to make a difference by speaking up. Student voice at its finest!

He taught me one of the leadership qualities every successful superintendent must possess: the ability to listen. When tech giant Google embarked on a massive research project aimed at determining how to build the perfect team, its findings confirmed what Yonatan Zunger learned during his time there: "In the best teams, members listen to one another and show sensitivity to each other's feelings and needs." [20]

Was Anton part of my "team"? Yes, absolutely! When we say that educating the Whole Child means tending to head, heart, and hands, we should add that Whole Child education is reciprocal, a meeting of the minds between adults and children in an atmosphere of mutual respect. How can we prepare our youth to meet the challenges of adulthood if we hold them at arm's length, lecture to them from afar, don't make them feel like they matter, don't believe in them, and don't involve them in decisions affecting their education?

The urgency of a learning environment that highlights reciprocity was brought home to me recently in two articles from the alumni magazine of Deerfield Academy in Massachusetts, where I went to high school. The first article identified the six critical qualities of an ideal Deerfield student:

1. Discipline

2. Collaboration

3. Resilience

4. Independence and initiative

5. Creativity

6. Curiosity

According to the author, these qualities—essential for twenty-first-century learning — are cultivated through methodologies known as design thinking and systems thinking. The former, derived from

---

[20] Charles Duhigg, "What Google Learned From Its Quest to Build the Perfect Team," *The New York Times,* Magazine, The Work Issue, February 25, 2016, https://www.nytimes.com/2016/02/28/magazine/what-google-learned-from-its-quest-to-build-the-perfect-team.html?_r=1.

commercial product design, promotes creativity and a trial-and-error approach, while the latter is a discipline that values an overarching analytical framework. Together, they generate these six ideal qualities in students, and, the article claimed, lay the foundation for successful participation in our highly technological, rapidly changing world.

While I recognize the relevance of these six qualities to a student's learning journey, something about them nagged at me. Flipping the pages of the magazine, I came upon an address to the school by renowned legal scholar (and Deerfield alumnus) Frank I. Michelman. A few words jumped out at me instantly: individualism, pluralism, unity, and fairness.

In his talk to the Deerfield community, Professor Michelman asserted that liberal values —"liberal" in the original meaning of "promoting economic and political freedoms"—balance the tension between the interests of the individual and society. Promoting unity among many, they ensure the fair application of laws. At their core, these values uphold mutual respect among a nation's people and protect scientific and intellectual inquiry from undue pressure and bias.

As I absorbed his words, I knew instantly what was missing from the six traits. All six could be in play, yet to ensure mutual respect and pluralism, to combat bias and uphold fairness, a seventh trait is needed: empathy.

Isn't empathy inherent in collaboration, you might ask? Doesn't curiosity breed empathy? At first glance, perhaps, but consider how many clusters of male scientists have worked collaboratively. . .yet excluded women. Think of the children in all-white neighborhoods whose avid curiosity ends where the "bad neighborhood" begins.

Our world is shaped by the digital revolution, yes, but also by economic inequality, racial injustice, and global warming. If design thinking and systems thinking aren't combined with empathy as we confront these challenges, our technology will amount to little more than fancy accessories available to the few. Viewing the world from a different perspective—walking in another's shoes—is not optional; in our complex, interdependent world, it is imperative.

Just as Google (re)discovered that teams of professionals thrive when members have sensitivity to each other's needs, so my time in

Sacramento taught me the importance of sensitivity, of empathy, to the development of healthy and successful young adults.

School superintendents are called to lead not one team, but many. They lead their staff, they lead the district, and most importantly—if they're doing their job right—they are the voice for all the children in their district. So, I guess it's lucky that the very same leadership skill is central to each dynamic: listening. When we listen to our staff, our stakeholders, and our children, we do more than enable ourselves and our colleagues to excel. We model the reciprocity and compassion that today's and tomorrow's professionals must cultivate to be successful and contribute to the world.

Leadership and Shared Vision: Project Green

While not every school district in the country faces challenges like Sacramento's, public schooling is a tough field. Every school superintendent will be tested, whether by insufficient funding, a hostile legislative environment, an entrenched educational bureaucracy, or a community conflicted over vouchers, charter schools, and the purpose of public education. Realistically speaking, most will confront all these and more.

Successful superintendents come from a variety of backgrounds. Some are lifelong educators and others take up the cause of public education after other careers. Yet all of them must have one leadership quality in common, which my interaction with young Anton also underscored: the ability (and tenacity) to create a shared vision that inspires everyone—students, parents, educators, and the community.

Creating a compelling vision is a powerful force. With vision, leaders set the direction that enables others to "see." We have to believe it before we can see it. Michelangelo spoke of such belief when he said, "I saw the angel in the stone and carved to set it free."

Implicit in Michelangelo's words is the urgency of turning vision into action. When Anton and his classmates created an opportunity for us to respond to an important environmental issue—getting rid of Styrofoam trays—they also pointed to a more compelling vision for our school district and community.

The "angel" they revealed to me was about educating and developing the Whole Child. It means creating challenging and relevant courses, promoting college and career-themed pathways, and making our schools and classrooms greener, healthier, and more sustainable places to work and learn.

Leaders who create a shared vision open possibilities, provide energy, and enable change to be more easily assimilated within their organizations. In Sacramento, for example, we easily could have stuck to "solving problems." We certainly had enough: aging facilities, declining budgets, low graduation rates, and too few children performing at grade level in math, language arts, and science. Instead, we found the extra gear that allowed us to not only solve problems, but also stay focused on the vision of what we wanted to create, what Peter Senge in his book *The Fifth Discipline* calls "creative tension."

Having a shared vision requires leaders to know themselves better and push themselves to new heights—to be their best and bring their best. For me, that meant allowing myself to be inspired by Anton, to build a vision of a school district that operated sustainably, and find the right moment for bold action beyond just eliminating Styrofoam trays.

It came during 2010, when I traveled to Sundance, Utah, to the first (and only) Green School Summit sponsored by the Redford Institute. Over a dozen city leaders from around the country were invited to come explore how to "green" their schools. Thanks to Sacramento Mayor Kevin Johnson's Greenwise Initiative, he and I were among the city mayors and school superintendents in attendance.

The Summit challenged us to think boldly. What would we do differently when we returned home? To inspire our thinking, we were offered an incentive to devise a plan to "green" our schools: The top two plans would be assigned a "Green School Fellow" for two years, all expenses paid, to assist with implementation.

Despite being the oldest school district west of the Mississippi, Sacramento hadn't passed a bond measure to support schools in a decade. Our facilities were worn and tired. What could we do that was daring, that would inspire our community to support a fresh bond measure and nurture the growing movement to give students more voice? It was in Sundance that Sacramento's Project Green was born.

Under the program, students from campuses throughout the school district would form "Green Teams" that, supported by parents and school staff, would conduct "green audits" of their schools. Working with professionals, the teams would draft recommendations for improvements, such as installing solar tubes to help light classrooms or adopting water-wise plumbing fixtures to save on California's most precious and threatened resource. A panel of community leaders from local environmental nonprofits and sustainable businesses would judge the plans during an Earth Day presentation event, and the most promising proposals would be awarded funding from a pool of remaining redevelopment funds.

Our Sundance sponsors loved the proposal and awarded us one of two Green School Fellows (the other went to the Boston Public Schools). Our school board was thrilled because they'd been asking to see evidence of our bond and redevelopment dollars at work. Several of our schools, like Theodore Judah Elementary, were already experimenting with school gardens and other "green" efforts and jumped at the chance to further engage their students and families. If done well, Project Green would position the school district to seek an additional bond measure in the fall of 2012.

The Green Fellow who was assigned to us, Farah McDill, gave a huge boost to our efforts, recruiting schools and organizing teams, finding community and business leaders to sit on our panel of judges, and overseeing the daily operation of the greening projects. Farah even brought us a project that enabled one of our most environmentally engaged teachers to bring a student on an excursion to Antarctica!

Project Green reflected a shared vision of Whole Child education in so many ways. First, the students worked independently and in teams, learning to collaborate, communicate, create, and connect emotionally to the projects they were working on and learning from. Second, the adults closest to them—their parents and teachers—worked with them, in support of their ideas and mission. Third, the green audits were focused on something bigger than passing a test or learning long division: the children were learning to apply their skills to a real-world problem and to serve the larger community.

I'll always remember the night of the project presentations. Students from Will C. Wood Middle School explained the thermal properties of glass. Another team, all elementary school students from various grades wearing jackets and ties and dresses, took turns presenting their project. One team member — probably a third grader — wore a suit with store tags still on the sleeve!

And the best part: several of our schools received grants of up to $500,000 in redevelopment funds to implement their plans. We spent the summer of 2011 working on the projects, placing special focus on engaging our buildings and grounds team. We really wanted our maintenance staff to feel like part of the education process. These efforts, in turn, attracted a new leader for buildings and grounds, Cathy Allen, who enthusiastically built upon our work, energizing her team through opportunities to support Project Green in tangible ways.

And remember our old friend Anton? He and his sister led a team that devised a plan for their school's bathrooms to be upgraded with energy-efficient appliances and fixtures. The day the two of them showed me around their school, they beamed with pride.

For Anton and his fellow students, Project Green was bigger than greening schools. And while it did help pave the way for a successful multimillion-dollar bond campaign in the fall of 2012, it was bigger even than that. Its true significance was that, for many students, Project Green marked the first time in their lives they could see that what they thought and created really mattered. It's impossible to overestimate the residual power of this experience.

Leadership and Shared Vision: Small Schools and Beyond

During my time in Charlotte, when that school board member told me "hope is not a strategy," my boss Pete and I agreed that hope may not be a strategy, but it is an essential ingredient to creating a vision. It's up to leaders of a school district or campus to help teams and the community believe that the work they do makes a difference. Inspiring people to imagine what is possible is critical to keeping them motivated and ensuring they stay the course.

When author Peter Senge was asked to share his definition of leadership, he said it comes down to two words: truth and love. The concept of truth ties back to listening and a willingness to be honest about where things currently are. The concept of love ties back to vision, to the idea that you love your vision so much, you are willing to be honest about where you currently are.

We need superintendents and school leaders who are so driven by their passion for educating children, "so inspired by love," that they craft a vision powerful enough to make them brutally honest about the current conditions of their schools and school districts. This capacity for self-reflection is critical. My own brutal reality in Sacramento was that to meet the diverse needs of disadvantaged children, "good" was never going to be good enough. We needed to be great to overcome the barriers these students faced daily and to fulfill the challenge issued to me during my first one hundred days in Sacramento: "Superintendent, take risks for kids."

I earlier described the vision around our Priority Schools—that during the height of the school funding crisis in California, we could transform several of our schools serving some of our neediest children in our most disadvantaged and distressed communities. By so doing, we would create beacons of hope and sites for experimentation, innovation, and excellence.

My vision for the district was also inspired by a visit I paid to the Met Sacramento, established in 2002 as part of the District's Small Schools Initiative. Operated in partnership with the Big Picture Network, a worldwide network of schools, the Met approaches education "one kid at a time."

Its highly engaging learning environment includes classwork just three days a week; the other two are spent in individualized internships. Through these structured workplace experiences and small learning communities, students gain knowledge and skills, learn by doing, and can demonstrate their learning in multiple ways.

During my visit, I got to observe a quarterly exhibition where students shared what they'd learned in front of parents, peers, and teachers. There we were, in a vintage portable classroom at the back of a converted elementary school, observing a spirited and student-driven defense of learning. The level of engagement, inquiry, and demonstration of knowledge convinced me we needed to expand opportunities for our students that were designed to meet those teens where they were.

My experience at the Met that day became the driving force for ensuring our district offered a range of academic choices to our students and families, and it was an easy sell to our diverse community. Like most urban school districts, Sacramento had been losing students to surrounding communities for more than a decade. We lived in a capital city, where thousands of people commuted to interesting, challenging jobs each day. Why couldn't we offer more attractive, interesting, and challenging programs of learning? Why couldn't we replicate our existing programs, each with long waiting lists?

Schools like the Met convinced me that career-themed academies with engaging and relevant curricula connected to internships and workplace experiential learning opportunities could excite students. Further, these schools do a better job of preparing students for college, careers, and life.

Driven by this insight, we expanded programs focusing on career pathways from just eight to more than two dozen. We created a pre-K-12 International Baccalaureate curriculum as well as Hmong and Chinese immersion programs, and we converted schools to meet the community's demand for Waldorf and integrated thematic instruction, a learning theory aimed at encouraging students to make connections across multiple topics, skills, and points of view.

Over time, as we realized our vision, district graduation rates soared from 68 percent to 85 percent, and the dropout rate plunged from 23 percent to less than 6 percent. Our community had a lot to be proud of, even though we had so much more to do. Were our actions bold? Certainly, our economic context could have justified a "just survive" mentality. Instead, we chose to disrupt the *status quo*, bringing focus and a sense of urgency to what we were doing. It was hard but truly exhilarating work.

Sharing the Vision with America

If Americans are serious about transforming public education, we need to foster school leadership grounded in love and truth at the highest levels. Our leaders must be committed to listening deeply to their diverse constituencies and communities and willing to take the necessary risks. They must create a shared vision, and execute, manage, and deliver on bold plans.

Every community in America, as it looks to its educational leadership, should be asking the following questions:

- Are our leaders equipped to lead and manage change within their systems?

- Do they know themselves and understand how to develop a shared vision to unleash creativity?

- Can these leaders cultivate good listening skills? Can they suspend judgments and examine their own beliefs and experiences?

- Can they stimulate team dynamics characterized by a safe place for honest input and dialogue, where teammates listen to one another and are sensitive to each other's feelings and needs?

- Are they courageous and willing to do what is best for children?

- Can they lead with an open mind and an open heart, and truly empathize and walk in someone else's shoes?

- How can we best support these leaders to do this hard and essential work?

- Will we give them time and space to learn, grow, and fail, then pick up the pieces and try again?

Chapter 8

Family Matters

Adult Education: Benefiting the Community Benefits Its Children

Adult education featured strongly in how we engaged and empowered our families and community. Literacy, English language classes, and career and technical education were among the topics we taught. Why did we fight hard to protect these programs in the face of budget cuts? Why, in a climate hostile to spending on public schools for kids, did we insist on extending education to adults at all? The answer is essential to the larger issue of fixing public education, so let's explore it, starting back in California.

Two years after I left Sacramento, California Governor Jerry Brown proposed putting $500 million toward the state's Adult Education Block Grant. The Great Recession had nearly decimated adult education programs statewide, and in approving the Governor's measure, the legislature finally acknowledged the need to redress this harmful state of affairs. The Adult Education Block Grant supports programs similar to what we fought for in Sacramento. Aimed at disadvantaged adults, it features basic elementary and high school classes including reading, writing, and math, as well as apprenticeships and job- focused technical skills training.

In California, many adult students are immigrants seeking English language skills and technical training to provide for their families. Nationwide, the vast majority of adult learners also are parents or other primary caretakers of school-age children. The benefits of offering them education are greater than you might expect.

Yes, adults with high school diplomas are better providers: working full-time, they earn nearly $10,000 more per year than those lacking a high school education.[21]   And it goes without saying that higher earnings boost not just family income, but our nation's economy as well. But the dividends to children extend beyond an improvement to their material circumstances: According to the National Institutes of Health, a child's future academic success hinges most upon his or her mother's ability to read.[22]

This is an extremely important finding: *maternal literacy outweighs such factors as family income and neighborhood in determining a child's chances of succeeding in school.* In other words, when parents thrive, children thrive. Equally important, job skills and education correlate to better health in adults and their children. Families with higher education levels visit hospitals less often and see lower rates of chronic diseases such as asthma and diabetes.[23]

So, when I hear people argue that we can't afford to provide adult education to immigrants and other disadvantaged adults, my answer is: we can't afford not to. There are so many ways to do the math.

[21] Employment Projections: Unemployment rates and earning by educational attainment, 2016," US Department of Labor, Bureau of Labor Statistics, October 24, 2017, https://www.bls.gov/emp/ep_chart_001.htm.

[22] Improving Mothers' Literacy Skills May Be Best Way to Boost Children's Achievement," Eunice Kennedy Shriver National Institute of Child Health and Human Development, National Institutes of Health, October 25, 2010, https://www.nichd.nih.gov/news/releases/102510-reading-family-income.

[23] "Quick Guide to Health Literacy," US Department of Health and Human Services, Office of Disease Prevention and Health Promotion, 2004, https://health.gov/communication/literacy/quickguide/factsliteracy.htm.

Economically, the McGraw-Hill Research Foundation reports that for every 400,000 adults earning a high school diploma, our nation gains $2.5 billion in tax revenues and lower spending.[24] In terms of public safety, adult education lowers recidivism in the prison population by close to 30 percent. Civic participation rises with education, too.[25]

If only our leaders dealt in facts and not in scare tactics that pit one group of Americans against another. We have the means to make our country richer, safer, more inclusive, and more equal. When we recite the Pledge of Allegiance, we promise loyalty to a nation that is "indivisible, with liberty and justice for all."

Indivisible means undivided, and liberty and justice are mere words unless we commit to the kind of freedom and fairness that come with economic opportunity. I could not stand by and allow Sacramento's adult education programs to be dismantled any more than I would let our children go to school without access to healthy food.

Parental Involvement and Empowerment: A Key to Success

Adult learners with school-age children pursue education in part to serve as better role models for their kids. They care deeply about their children's schoolwork, and contrary to the prevailing stereotypes, studies show that parental engagement knows no race or income level: disadvantaged parents have the same degree of involvement in their children's education as their wealthier peers.[26]

A major obstacle to family involvement across the board is communication. Absent a true partnership between schools and families, a gap forms between parents and teachers and each side is hampered

---

[24] Lennox McLendon, Debra Jones, and Mitch Rosin, "The Return on Investment (ROI) From Adult Education and Training: Measuring the Economic Impact of a Better Educated and Trained U.S. Workforce," McGraw-Hill Research Foundation http://www.iacea.net/wp-content/docs/ROI_Adult_Education_Report.pdf.

[25] Stephen J. Steurer and Linda G. Smith, "Education Reduces Crime: Three-State Recidivism Study," Correctional Education Association and Management & Training Corporation Institute, 2003, http://www.mtctrains.com/wp-content/uploads/2017/06/Education-Reduced-Crime-Three-State-Recidivism-Study.pdf.

[26] Chuck Dervarics and Eileen O'Brien, "Back to school: How parent involvement affects student achievement," Center for Public Education, August 30, 2011, http://www.centerforpubliceducation.org/Main-Menu/Public-education/Parent-Involvement/Parent-Involvement.html.

by a lack of knowledge about goals and expectations for students in the classroom and at home.

In Sacramento, we worked hard to bridge that gap through campaigns that welcomed parents to our schools and built trust between families and educators. Efforts like this pay off: regardless of income level, children whose parents take an active interest in their education get better grades, have an easier time socially, and are more likely to graduate from high school and pursue higher learning.[27]

The most valuable parental involvement programs focus on family support of learning in the home. This was so important that we focused a third of our strategic plan on engaging our community. Our Welcoming Schools certification encouraged campuses to build ties with families. The community review process allowed parents to evaluate their school's climate and culture. Parent Leadership Academies focused the whole community on student success and prepared and empowered parents for leadership opportunities throughout the community. One of our school board members, Christina Pritchett, started this way. And our Whole Child, Whole Day, Whole Year approach defied the prevailing trend to close schools to conserve energy and instead surrounded our children with opportunities for growth.

I remain proud that in Sacramento, we focused explicitly on building relationships with our parents and families through the Parent Teacher Home Visit Project I described in chapter three. Instead of leaving it to chance, we made nurturing relationships with parents, our most important partners, a top priority.

We didn't stop there. Building on these relationships, we empowered our families to participate actively in their child's learning through Academic Parent Teacher Teams. Our teachers invited parents into the classroom not just to catch them up on their children's progress, but to encourage them to set goals for their kids at home and to provide training and exercises to bring the family together around homework assignments and other learning-centered activities.

This is why our Priority Schools were so important. In times of significant financial stress, they provided havens to be bold and try new strategies. Instead of letting the difficult times be an excuse,

---

[27] Ibid.

we took advantage of the opportunity to build community, literally opening our schools and bringing parents, families, and the community into our classrooms. Think how powerful a child's experience of school can be when parents, families, and teachers are linked arm in arm in the learning process.

One of the country's heroes of parental involvement is Michele Brooks, who for seven years was assistant superintendent at the Boston Public Schools' Office of Family and Student Engagement. An outsider to the field of education, Brooks became passionate about parental involvement for one simple reason: as a parent of three who'd moved her children from Tennessee to Massachusetts so they could access the excellent education she'd gotten in Boston decades earlier, she quickly noticed that her kids were not being challenged or encouraged to succeed.

An IT specialist, Brooks started volunteering at her daughter's high school, creating a resource center for parents to network and organize. Soon, she founded the Boston Parents Organizing Network, which advocated for school funding and quality education. From there, Brooks was appointed to the school board and eventually became an assistant superintendent.

Her overriding mission was to tie parental involvement to the district's academic goals. By strategically aligning family engagement with educational improvement, she "moved the work of her office from a peripheral activity to one that is central to the needs of the district's 57,000 students and their families."[28] Today, her approach serves as a model for school districts everywhere.

To me, it's no coincidence that Michele Brooks was a parent, a graduate of public schools, and an outsider to the education bureaucracy. As a parent, she had real passion for improving the schools her children attended and personally understood the power of family engagement. As someone who'd succeeded in life because of public education, she had no patience for narratives of failure. Brooks expected her children to receive a first-class education without abandoning the public school system. And as an outsider, she brought a fresh perspective

---

[28] Michele Molnar, "Boston Leader Connects Parents to Learning," EdWeek, February 4, 2013, http://www.edweek.org/ew/articles/2013/02/06/20ltlf-brooks.h32.html.

untainted by years of struggle in a system that can instill fatigue and disappointment, often leading to a sense of resignation.

Not every parent will one day be recruited to help run their children's schools in a paid position. However, in schools that create a path for families to get engaged, that build trust and a welcoming environment, all parents have a role to play both in supporting their children's education and in improving their schools.

Again, the question of leadership arises: teachers and administrators who set aside defensiveness, are willing to listen and be humble when challenged, are willing to visit parents on their terms and in their homes, and openly welcome the community into their schools and classrooms will reap the rewards of meaningful partnerships with families. Those families will, in turn, fight the good fight for funding and excellence with their district and state leaders instead of fighting against them. This is how we build community for its most fundamental purpose—supporting, educating, and developing children.

Chapter 9

A Vision Unleashed

Whole Child Education: A Close-Up View

Wherever it thrives, Whole Child education quickly shows skeptics that besides meeting the needs of children, the Whole Child movement reaps its own rewards, bringing forth all the assets children offer their communities and families when they're nurtured, supported, and educated holistically. Want to see for yourself? Accompany me on a visit to Esteban E. Torres High School in East Los Angeles, one of twelve "partner schools" working with the Los Angeles Education Partnership (LAEP), a Stuart Foundation partner.

Arriving at this two-acre campus, home to five pilot schools called "academies," it's easy to see the role students play in this unique urban educational setting. Their voices call loudly from every nook and cranny. Since 2010, these teacher-designed schools have served their surrounding community, predominately Hispanic and poor, delivering a graduation rate of 87 percent among students who often are the first in their families to finish high school and go to college. By comparison, California's statewide graduation rate is 81 percent, and LA's is 74 percent.

The Humanitas Academy of Arts and Technology features a "College Wall" displaying college acceptance letters, now considered the epitome of cool. Student self-portraits and other art work from a recent show hang nearby. Everywhere you look, you see and feel learning—and the confidence that comes with it.

"We want them to walk across that stage at graduation with their high school diploma in one hand and a college acceptance letter in the other," says Cristina Patricio, LAEP's community schools coordinator.

Former Torres High School student Guadalupe, the first in her family to graduate from college, recently returned to working in the school store and encourages girls and young women like her to stick with it. "It's her chance to give back," Patricio explains. For Guadalupe, the key to her success was simple: The size of the school and the relationship she had with her teachers made this place feel like home.

Meanwhile, at the Performing Arts Magnet, orchestra students who'd never picked up a violin or cello before the ninth grade are playing in an ensemble. They practice for ninety minutes each day while also learning about the history and language of music. "Here, all our students perform," Principal Carolyn MacKnight explains.

While only a handful go on to performing arts colleges, Performing Arts Magnet students find their voice as engineers, entrepreneurs, and doctors. "When a student can be passionate about learning something ninety minutes a day, it opens them up to other possibilities," says Principal MacKnight.

LAEP's vision is to foster educational excellence in Los Angeles County's high-poverty, multicultural communities through student empowerment, community engagement, school autonomy, and valuing teachers as professionals. Echoing LAEP's values, the academies place the needs and interests of their students at the center of teaching and learning. You won't hear the traditional end-of-period bells; each academy sets its own schedule. What they have in common are student-led parent and family conferences, where parents get to witness their children as learners and discuss their educational experience.

All the academies are organized by "advisories," small groups of students supported by the same teacher for four years, which give them time to build a rapport and get to know their students. Perhaps most importantly, the academies attract teachers who pride themselves on working together to hone their profession and to support and challenge their students. Here, good is not good enough.

"Students notice and respond when adults change their behaviors to be responsive to their needs," says Ellen Pais, LAEP's CEO.

"Having a voice in student court is important," a student from the Social Justice Leadership Academy comments. "There is one student who told me she is president of her tenth-grade class like I was, and wants to be president in eleventh grade, too. She wants to be a mini-me!" He beams as he says this.

Next to him, another student shares an idea: "I think as students we should be allowed to vote at sixteen. We should have a say in how our schools are run and how money is spent before we graduate." Wow!

These students are invested both in their futures and in their school community. Trusted by adults and empowered with agency over their learning environments, these students are ready to advocate for themselves and their peers.

Giving Students a Voice

We often talk about "silver bullets" in education, yet in truth there aren't any. What Torres and schools like it make clear is the importance of helping students have a voice in their education. From student-led conferences to curricula and teaching that engage, challenge, and awaken their creativity and passion to lowering the voting age for school board elections, all these ideas build on one another, adding up to Whole Child, student-centered learning that lets our young people find their voice. Where students have a voice, you find energy, curiosity, motivation, and learning. [29]

---

[29] Heather Staker, "How to Create Higher Performing, Happier Classrooms in Seven Moves," Christensen Institute, https://www.christenseninstitute.org/wp-content/uploads/2017/01/How-to-create-higher-performing-happier-classrooms-in-seven-moves.pdf.

Student-centered learning received a major boost with the December 2015 passage of Every Student Succeeds Act (ESSA). Under the leadership of then-Secretary of Education John King, ESSA replaced No Child Left Behind, finally giving states the latitude to pursue Whole Child education in earnest. Having lost both his parents at an early age, King acted from his first-hand experience of having his mind, body, and spirit nurtured in a supportive school environment.

For those of us who believe that education is more than test scores and double blocks of math, ESSA is cause for optimism. But let's not kid ourselves. American education is full of fads, the textbook and testing businesses (which are billion-dollar businesses) have a vested interest in the status quo, and changing faces in the White House and beyond can radically alter education policy and priorities with the stroke of a pen.

If the Whole Child approach is to weather the storm of shifting public education priorities, it must first be recognized for what it is. Whole Child is not a menu or checklist: "Healthy lunches, check." "After-school program, check." It's not just about more libraries, art classes, school nurses, and summer programs, though it certainly includes these supports. First and foremost, it's about beliefs.

Whole Child educators view every child as unique, gifted, and deserving of the opportunity to reach her fullest potential. We have an urgent commitment to classes that excite students and teachers alike, because both must be engaged for real learning to take place. We encourage every child to create, write, publicly speak, think, organize, draw, and paint. As former Secretary King emphasized, arts education and creativity are integral to learning and teaching. Moreover, we question whether multiple-choice tests can measure what our children know and how our children are progressing both as students and as human beings.

High-stakes tests can perpetuate the cycle of failure by keeping children from experiencing success. Performance assessments where students demonstrate mastery of subject matter and material deliver a very different experience and message. Some students have to take them several times to pass. Think of the incentives and signals we send when this is how we judge mastery and readiness for career, college, and life. Implicit in "go do it again" are signals that say *you matter, we believe in you, we are pushing you, you can do this, don't quit!*

The Whole Child approach is about educating the heart and the hands as well as the head, enabling children to believe in themselves, to know and say out loud what excites them, challenges them, and scares them. It means championing empathy and compassion, empowering parents through home visits, providing healthy and nutritious foods and time to enjoy them, and offering dental care, medical care, and social services to kids whose families can't access or afford them. Our children come to school with so many needs. We must meet them where they are, give them a say, and listen to their voices. We must encourage flexible thinking and emotional intelligence.

In a world as complex and fast-paced as our own, we must prepare students with the creativity, confidence, and emotional resilience to tackle problems, confront difficult realities, and meet new challenges head on.

Life long Learner

Chapter 10

The Real Cost of Underfunding

Whole Child Programs: First to Go

According to the traditional view of education, what matters most are reading, writing and 'rithmatic. Today, you'd have to add "really good app design skills" to the all-important three "R's," but the principle is still the same: teach our children content and an easily defined set of skills out of a mass-produced 400-plus-page textbook. Everything else is just icing on the cake.

Now think about twenty-first-century jobs. Required skill sets change all the time. If you're an IT specialist, for example, the hardware you work on evolves on every year and the "cloud technology" that didn't exist when you got your first promotion is the biggest thing going—for now. In five years the cloud will be close to obsolete, and something equally monumental will have taken its place.

Having a particular set of skills isn't what matters; *the ability to learn new skills* is far more relevant to success today. What are the characteristics of a lifelong learner? Empathy, flexibility, communications skills (especially listening), curiosity and questioning, and resilience all come to mind—the same skills Yonatan Zunger had to learn as an engineer. And how do we acquire those traits? Surely not by memorizing facts and figures dictated to us from the front of a classroom.

Does that mean children don't need to learn content or shouldn't receive academic instruction? Of course not. I don't know a single educator or policy expert who argues against the three, four, or five R's. What I do hear from many highly respected leaders in the field, such as Sir Ken Robinson, is that success in school and in life requires more, and that our children are far better positioned for achievement when educators treat them like the whole human beings they are.

Because traditional thinking is stubbornly resistant to new findings and evolving socioeconomic realities, when school budgets get cut, Whole Child programs are the first to go. At a time when the only thing we know about the future of work is that it's unknown—when technological advances have made memorization obsolete and creativity and critical thinking essential for many white-collar jobs—the default sadly is to cut the programs that develop these essential capacities: summer and after-school programs, art, music, band, wood shop, vocational classes, athletics, and even electives such as debate and robotics.

A Crisis in Funding

Educating the Whole Child requires funding for our teachers to advance their craft through continuous development. It requires empowering parents and families to create a network of support for children, and it requires resources so there are enough adults present in schools and school districts to attend to more than just students' academic needs: adults with enough time, bandwidth, and training to both listen and respond. In short, attending to the Whole Child means that the government, and the taxpayers who support it, must insist that the interest of children be placed at the center of their decisions and funded accordingly, with great attention to intention.

I say "in short" knowing full well how long the road really is. To quote the US Army Corps of Engineers during WWII, "The difficult we can do immediately; the impossible will take a little longer."

In terms of fiscal fundamentals, success in education is no different than in business or in the nonprofit world: you have to hire people hungry to learn and improve and work to ensure they have the knowledge, skills, and tools to better their craft. How far off the mark is our country when it comes to supporting public education? In the summer of 2016, the *Wall Street Journal* reported that in several states, lawmakers were struggling to ensure that schools would even open on time.[30] According to US News & World Report, in 2016, at least twenty-fivestates—including California—were spending less per student than before the 2008 recession.[31]

During the 2008 recession—the most precipitous revenue decline since the 1920s—leaders in California had to make very difficult choices. What gets funded and what gets cut? Having run an urban school district during that time, I have a serious critique of California's lawmakers for not doing enough to protect and support public education. While it's true that they worked alongside Governor Brown to mitigate the worst damage to schools by raising taxes to support education and public safety during this period, they did not do nearly enough. As they approached their school budget reductions, they took an axe to a forest that, even before the recession, had already been severely thinned.

Today, schools in California—like those in so many states—are still treading water. It's not that people in power are motivated by a desire to cut education funding. It's more that we don't have a model that builds sufficient political will and organizes the entire community around data-driven, persuasive arguments for how to fund our schools for success. Consequently, inadequate funding remains an

[30] Melissa Korn, Douglas Belkin, Kris Maher, "Funding Fights Vex School Districts," *The Wall Street Journal*, Education, June 5, 2016, https://www.wsj.com/articles/funding-fights-vex-school-districts-1465167221.

[31] Lauren Camera, "America's Bankrupt Schools," *US News and World Report*, March 18, 2016, https://www.usnews.com/news/the-report/articles/2016-03-18/why-big-city-school-systems-are-going-broke.

underlying issue across the country. We need courage from policy makers at every level to address it. We need courage among the public as well: recognition that even if you don't have kids in schools, it is in your interest, as a citizen, to support stronger investment in public education.

Let's face it. If you worry about high crime, or a faltering economy, or a country splintering around class, race, and other differences, what you're really worrying about is poor educational outcomes and the many negative consequences that come with our lack of investment in public education.

It's not just about overcrowded classrooms, closed libraries, cancelled music classes, and shortages of qualified teachers, principals, and superintendents. All those individual deficits add up to a system that cannot function to serve the community. Our deficits are a testament to our own lack of focus, our poor planning, and a blurring of priorities. They point to a society that addresses the education and development of its children with passivity instead of urgency.

In Carroll County, Mississippi, the school superintendent actually gave up his salary to help address the "wretched conditions" of his rural school district.[32]

"Like a city under siege," Superintendent Billy Joe Ferguson wrote in an open letter to Mississippi's governor, "our school district is surviving on limited resources and hope."[33] Unable to hire experienced teachers or purchase new textbooks, Ferguson wasn't asking for iPads or state-of-the-art facilities, just the basics that would allow the 1,000 children in his district to learn: "There is no excuse for not giving us at least enough money to just be adequate."

In Sacramento, meanwhile, Eric Chapman, principal at Sacramento's Harkness Elementary, came in on weekends to wash floors and motivated community partners such as the organization 100 Black Men of America, Inc., to donate resources and become mentors to children.

---

[32] Kayleigh Skinner, "Q & A: Mississippi superintendent explains why he gave up his salary to help relieve 'wretched conditions' at his schools," *The Hechinger Report*, February 2, 2015, http://hechingerreport.org/q-a-mississippi-superintendent-explains-why-he-gave-up-his-salary-to-help-relieve-wretched-conditions-at-his-schools/.

[33] Billy Joe Ferguson, "Open Letter to Governor Phil Bryant," January 21, 2015, http://www.mpe.org/mpe/pdf/newsletterPDF/BSBJ.Ferguson.OpenLtr.012215.pdf.

Throughout our schools and communities, thousands of men and women like Eric and Billy Joe do all they can for our children. They deserve leaders willing to have their backs, remove obstacles in their paths, and commit to getting them the tools and resources they need to do their work well.

From North Carolina to New York to Wyoming, courts evaluating flawed state funding formulas have confirmed what any pragmatic, nonideological observer will tell you: Schools that are under-resourced tend to fail their children and their communities, while schools that are well-funded produce more students prepared to contribute to their communities and to society.[34]

Playing the blame game won't solve anything. You can argue the underfunding is caused by ballooning teacher pensions, money diverted to charter schools, plummeting property values, or wealthy elected officials unconcerned about schools that serve the poor. But while we're busy pointing fingers, another generation of children is drifting along, feeling alienated or ignored, struggling to find meaning in school, or just plain dropping out. So even as we advocate for more resources in the future, we must focus on educating kids today, right now.

Thinking Creatively About Supporting Education

While the resource issues are real, public school systems could do more with what they have if their entire communities were involved in crafting innovative models for educational success. The Whole Child philosophy, properly understood, extends outward to redefine the concepts of community and caring for children. If the Whole Child is at the center, and the school forms a ring of support, what constitutes the wider rings of community surrounding child and school? The third and outer ring has to be both the public and private sectors, especially the latter with its keen interest in an educated workforce.

---

[34] Valerie Strauss, "How grossly underfunded are public schools?" *The Washington Post*, Education, November 25, 2012, https://www.washingtonpost.com/news/answer-sheet/wp/2012/11/25/how-grossly-underfunded-are-public-schools/?utm_term=.c6028432ee63.

Increasingly, this sector is defined by innovation, curiosity, and imagination, and stands to benefit hugely from expanded SEL programs that develop these skills in students from an early age.

Thus, the time has come to breathe life into the inherent reciprocity between private enterprise and the education system: the digital revolution needs creative, versatile, self-motivated workers, and our schools need active, engaged partnerships with the leaders of our innovative and creative economies.

What do you think of when you hear "innovation"? I've always associated it with people like Steve Jobs and Bill Gates, so naturally, when I was superintendent in Sacramento, I wrote Bill Gates a letter requesting his support for an "innovative" idea. I didn't ask him for money, but rather for a commodity of perhaps greater value: his time, and a brain trust of his colleagues, to leverage the funding we already had to create better schools.

As a fan of manual transmissions, I said, I know first gear is designed for one thing: to get the car moving. I likened charter schools to first gear. Part of their original purpose was to get the education system going, to shake up the status quo and offer families and students new options.

In exchange for certain freedoms and flexibility—limited oversight from elected school boards, minimal collective bargaining obligations—charter schools were supposed to try new approaches, serve as sites of innovation, and then share these ideas and practices with the entire public education system. What good is innovation if it's relegated to a single classroom, school, or group of schools? What good is innovation if we can't replicate, scale, and spread what works?

With few exceptions, instead of sharing out new and effective classroom practices and ways to engage families and empower and lift up communities, charter schools became islands of isolation. In fact, in many communities, charter schools have become the destination—the "competition"—with plans to create dozens, even hundreds more, as if this will magically cure what ails public education.

Fortunately, select charter organizations such as Envision Schools and Big Picture Schools in the San Francisco Bay Area, Green Dot in Los Angeles County, and Samueli Academy in Orange County, California, are working closely with their public school counterparts, sharing practices such as performance assessments and portfolio defenses that are working so well in their handful of schools.

The usual public education approach to scaling, I explained to Gates, is to test a few ideas, a.k.a., "pilots" or "early adopters." If we just copy and put some money behind them, we can create the scale and spread we desire. Instead of wondering why that approach fails — and it usually does — or doubting the efficacy of the innovative program or practice itself, what if we engaged the business community to help us understand the complexities of scaling?

Successful businesses understand the complicated barriers to replicating, scaling, and spreading good models. They understand how to anticipate the challenges that will inevitably arise when they look to scale and grow. That's what inspired my letter: I asked Gates to convene a group of his friends and colleagues to explore the replication of innovative educational approaches while key education leaders sat in attendance to listen, learn, and ask questions.

Finally, I thought, we could start to truly understand innovation, which, if it means anything, has to mean spreading new and effective approaches on a meaningful scale — moving us from first gear to fifth. More than ever, we need to forge partnerships across sectors so children benefit from the best thinking available.

Perhaps it won't surprise you that I never heard back. If you're reading this, Bill, it's never too late. Meanwhile, all of us at the Stuart Foundation are plowing ahead, nurturing the innovation and public-private partnerships we believe will make the difference. Are more dollars needed to better fund schools? Yes! There is so much more we could do to nurture and mentor our young people: to support art, music and drama classes, and librarians, counselors, nurses, and music teachers. Because children continue to show up at school on Monday mornings, we can't sit still. All of us — superintendents, parents, teachers and principals, and community members — need to be much more clear-eyed, articulate, and persuasive about why more investment in children's education matters and what we might get in return. Change can happen. It takes time, and it must start at the local grassroots level.

Chapter 11

An Action Plan and a Case Study to Help Us Move Forward

I'm often asked what steps can be taken to advance the Whole Child agenda and make our public school system revolve around the real needs of students and families. Understandably, people want a game plan, even though each local school board, each state legislature, each nationwide initiative poses unique challenges and requires specific forms of intervention.

To provide a helpful road map, I have identified two common themes useful to all stakeholders — parents, teachers, policy makers, etc. — and outlined roles and strategies that each separate category of stakeholder should find useful. As a companion to the action plan, I have offered a case study in reimagining schools to illustrate what it takes to transform a school into a Whole Child–centered community of learning.

My Action Plan for Change
For All Stakeholders: Adopt the Model of Structural Change

Whether you're the parent of a kindergarten student or a school principal with ten years under her belt, I urge you to step back from the particular challenge you're facing and consider how it connects to the big picture. While you and your community may not always have the leverage to change the big picture, you'll have zero chance to do so if you're only focused on the problem at hand.

I've offered several examples of how the school system can function like that carnival game Whack-A-Mole, where you hit one stuffed animal on the head with a mallet only to have another one pop up elsewhere. Ask teachers to participate in more professional development and find yourself immersed in a conflict over who gets blamed for lower test scores in classrooms where teachers have been occasionally absent. . . to participate in professional development! Establish a network of schools that reward excellent teaching, and watch as a non-network campus becomes a magnet for bad teachers who want to avoid the high standards your new schools have set.

Approaching a problem structurally means anticipating those unexpected outcomes through careful analysis and input from all the people who stand to be affected. Let's say your neighborhood wants to create a small private kindergarten, whose teachers will be paid more than public school teachers, in exchange for a longer work day and a year-round teaching schedule. You can rush ahead with the plan, then find that your whole town hates you because all the best teachers have left the public school where most of their kids still go. Or you can begin by bringing in the community, including teachers, and explore options that would make your plan work for everyone involved.

Maybe it's about identifying great teachers who can't realistically work a longer day or need summers off and making sure they're incentivized to stay in the schools that serve your community. Maybe it's about sharing resources with parents about the new school and committing to help them advocate for better kindergartens throughout the district.

The point is to apply a wider lens to the problem in front of you. Just as the Whole Child approach considers the heart and the hands as well as the head, a structural analysis of the challenge you're facing will highlight its many angles and, most importantly, its wider context. Just as we welcomed families into our schools in Sacramento, forging bonds with the community where our work was taking place, your analysis needs a generous perspective on who will be affected by your plan.

If this advice feels exhausting, that's why taking on education must be a community-wide effort. One person alone, however resilient, can't do it. But the good news is, taking a structural approach will yield truly effective, sustainable outcomes. In the process of getting there, you'll create new relationships and bonds of trust you never imagined.

For All Stakeholders: Insist on Both/And, Not Either/Or

The moment change stops is when all the stakeholders take sides, retreating behind "I'm-right-therefore-you're-wrong" barricades. My one-time boss and mentor Pete Gorman puts it like this: "We get into these semantic battles, where if the teachers raise objections to an accountability metric, we say they don't care about kids. What a load of crap!"

We can't choose sides when it comes to our children. *Should we use data or hugs?* Come on, people, it can't be a war between metrics and love! To improve the lives of all public school students, we need both. It's never been more urgent to deploy and model both/and thinking, whether it's public education you're concerned with or the general state of the planet.

For Parents

My most important advice for parents is to get involved and stay active in your child's education any way you can. For some, this means asking your child some seemingly simple questions at the end of each day:

- What did you learn today?

- What classes, subjects, and activities are you enjoying and feeling challenged by?

- Are you getting the support you need to do well in school and feel good about being there?

Parents need to be armed with two pieces of knowledge. First, you know what your child needs. Don't let a jargon-filled school district plan intimidate you. If you don't like the answers you're hearing when you talk with your child about his or her school day, trust your gut.

Second, parents have more power than anyone else involved in public schools. If you knew the power you had, you'd be unstoppable. The school board works for you. Here's how the system operates: Your influence on the school board translates into the board's influence on the superintendent, who then takes your concerns to his or her school principals, who in turn can take action on the ground. I'm not offering an opinion on whether this hierarchical structure is ideal, but you have to know how it works. Only then can you make it work for you.

For parents who can make the time, it's important to assist with class projects and volunteer to participate in school activities. Remember, a school or district is a community. Communities need to be nourished and replenished. Waldorf schools, described in the case study you'll read soon, are a notable example. Parents help create and sustain a community around their children's school, adding a critical layer of support to students, teachers, and families.

My son was a Waldorf student, and when one of his classmates had a sick parent, other parents supported the family by giving rides to school, cooking and delivering meals, and shopping for groceries. Building this sense of community around a school is powerful. When the time comes, that community can be mobilized to advocate for the changes you seek.

Advocating for change can include lobbying the school board and becoming a leader who inspires others to be change makers. As we learned from Michele Brooks, an engaged parent can move mountains. From simply attending meetings of school site councils or parent associations to playing a role in their governance or even running for a school board seat, you as a parent can play the part that's right for you.

For Teachers

I knew so many dedicated teachers in Sacramento who were hungry for better methods to reach their students and eager to take risks to achieve a healthier, more supportive, better-performing school environment. Most teachers go into education with an innate passion for and commitment to supporting the growth of young minds, the evolution of young citizens, and the ultimate success of their students. It's a sadly well-known fact that the school system wears many of them down.

Chronically underpaying and disregarding teachers is societal self-destruction. These teachers deserve better, but I worry that however well-intentioned their union representatives may be, the standard calls for higher wages and better benefits (or protection of the pay and benefits they have now) are not a great match for what's happening in schools today. Because the budget wars aren't ending any time soon, what can teachers do to improve the way the job feels? How can they gain a deeper sense of satisfaction and accomplishment from their work?

Advocating for a Whole Child focus doesn't just benefit students and their families. When it gets right down to it, dedicated educators would be less angry about paying a bit more for healthcare if they got to consistently witness their students succeeding in school, attending college, and shaping successful lives. When students flourish, teachers blossom. Having a Whole Child focus has to begin with teacher wellness, which means teachers' unions should be pushing for school cultures that are conducive to the health and well-being of the adults working with children.

Teachers should rally for involvement in leadership and decision-making in their schools and for professional growth and learning opportunities that don't penalize them, but rather help them build new knowledge, skills, and tools that enable them to better support, engage, and connect with their students. They should seek more compensated time to collaborate with peers and colleagues. As

I witnessed in Sacramento, the process of trading tips and new information, sharing ideas, and working in teams makes the teaching profession more rewarding.

For Superintendents

This entire book can be a manual for superintendents committed to bringing the Whole Child approach to our schools. If I had two pieces of advice to offer every leader of a school district, it would be this: First, As I stated earlier, superintendents are in a unique position to make changes that can positively affect the lives of children. Embrace the opportunity. Second, superintendents need to recognize that they can't lead a Whole Child–focused system if they themselves aren't whole. Leadership begins on the inside.

Are you living with purpose? Are your beliefs and values clear? Are you clear on what you are—and are not—willing to do, even if it costs you your job? Are you being the change you want to see in the world? Spearheading a movement for change is a punishing proposition. Do you have some discipline or structure in your life (such as meditation) that enables you to pause, reflect, and rejuvenate? Interior wholeness can only be achieved when you have and maintain balance in your life. As Bill O'Brien, the late CEO of Hanover Insurance, said, "The success of the intervention is dependent on the interior state of the intervenor."

For Policy Makers

As I outlined in chapter two, the Whole Child approach to educating and developing children is not a new concept. Back at the dawn of American public education, schools applied a holistic lens to how children learn and develop, and to the skills and capabilities they need to become curious and inquisitive learners, community members, and leaders. Elected officials, school board trustees, and state and federal regulators must take heed of the historical data and the science behind this methodology, especially in light of its applicability to the jobs of the twenty-first century.

Please stop the "policy pendulum swings." Believe that educating children benefits when more control resides in communities. Focus on continuous improvement versus punitive accountability models. Advocate for and provide stable and adequate funding. To resist the Whole Child movement is to turn our backs on the future. Our nation's progress and place in the world rests on its ability to forge empathetic, collaborative, lifelong learners.

For Philanthropy

Having joined the ranks of funders myself, my best advice is to practice humility. Remember where the work and learning really take place: in classrooms, schools, and communities. Remember where the power really resides: on the ground with people doing the work. The power is not in the ivory tower, not in think tanks, not in K Street offices where education industry lobbyists gather. Your constituency is children. Students, families, and educators should define the core of your universe. Listen to them and partner with them. Step aside from the endless torrent of ideas, theories, and competing agendas and center your mission and grant making around the children.

A Case Study for Reimagining Schools

If you don't work in the field of education, you may not know the name Linda Darling-Hammond. But if you care about schools, you should. A noted Stanford professor, Linda is president and CEO of the Learning Policy Institute, an organization that conducts independent research aimed at reimagining schools and transforming K-12 education. When she turned her attention to Alice Birney School (formerly John Morse), a Waldorf-inspired public school in Sacramento, she asked to interview me to get my thoughts and recollections.

By the time we spoke, I'd been gone from Sacramento for over a year. Talking to Linda and exchanging perspectives on what Alice Birney has meant to its students, parents, and teachers put me on a path to rethinking its larger meaning. If a largely impoverished urban school district can cultivate and sustain an educational oasis, what are the implications for the movement to reimagine public schools?

Like the Superintendent's Priority Schools, Alice Birney operates with a unique curriculum and a belief that every student can succeed. Unlike the Priority Schools, this Waldorf-inspired school originated with teachers—a small group of motivated individuals who taught themselves the Waldorf method, then tirelessly advocated for a campus where they could apply what they'd learned.

Over time, the school faced a series of challenges in its relationship with parents, teachers, the district, and national policies such as Common Core. Thanks to the in-depth study conducted by Linda Darling-Hammond and her colleagues,[35] we can examine those important moments of tension and conflict and identify key components useful to all of us who are determined to reimagine schools and transform public education.

Revisiting the Waldorf model caused me to identify a new dimension to my belief that to transform education, we must first and foremost focus on children. While this philosophy applies to school curricula and lesson plans, to what we feed our kids in school and how we plan their summer activities, it also applies on the policy level. Given a chance to testify before Congress or have a one-on-one with the secretary of education, if they asked me how to reimagine our schools, I'd offer the advice: start with our children.

Inevitably, they'd bring up budgets. Are you on the side that says we're just throwing money at the problem, or the side that says we're starving our schools? I would politely shake my head and repeat: start with our children. What Alice Birney shows us is that when a school is organized around its children, a community—consisting of students, teachers, administrators, and families—is formed.

An authentic community—one built on mutual respect, on collaboration, on listening—speaks with a single voice. Once that voice is ready to speak, that's when we can talk about budget priorities. And instead of students who are at odds with teachers, who are at odds with administrators, who are at odds with parents, you will

[35] Diane Friedlaender, Kyle Beckham, Xinhua Zheng, and Linda Darling-Hammond. "Growing a Waldorf-Inspired Approach in a Public School District," Stanford Center for Opportunity Policy in Education, 2015, https://edpolicy.stanford.edu/sites/default/files/publications/scope-report-waldorf-inspired-school.pdf.

hear the voice of a community confident in the values we need to instill in education to prepare children not just for college and career, but for life. That's where budgeting should begin: not with a list of needed supplies or a staffing model, but with a set of values.

Imagine a legislature that can't play teachers off against administrators or administrators against parents because they're standing side by side, united around a values-driven budget that's not tied to one special interest or another, but instead is designed to support proven models of education that will move our country forward. On that day, change will happen—guaranteed.

Alice Birney: An Overview

You may recall my first impressions when, during my first one hundred days as superintendent, I visited John Morse, the Waldorf-Inspired school that later moved to the Alice Birney campus. It felt, looked, sounded, even smelled unlike every other school I'd visited. There were children's mud boots in the halls, along with the sounds of singing and of adult voices speaking in calm, modulated tones. There were natural plantings and wood play structures everywhere.

While all of this intrigued me, I didn't realize how deliberate the environment at John Morse was, or how it connected with a philosophy about child development and learning that's in direct opposition to the high-stakes testing approach shaping our educational system today. The values behind Waldorf schools are rooted in a belief system that—as described in the section entitled "The Whole Child in History"—goes back centuries. It sees the child as an individual, whose innate talents must be nurtured through freedom and compassion, not stifled by rules, punishments, and rigid, one-size-fits-all curricula that bear no relationship to the natural world.

To acquaint you with the Waldorf model, I'll start with a quote not from Rudolph Steiner, who invented Waldorf, but from Linda Darling-Hammond, whose words illustrate the urgency of applying a holistic, child-centric model to education: "If we taught babies to talk as most skills are taught in school, they would memorize lists of sounds in a predetermined order and practice them alone in a closet." Wow.

Think about what she's really saying about how children learn. Language acquisition is hard: ask any American adult who's struggled to master French or Mandarin. But our children are custom-built to acquire language. In fact, any interference from education "experts" would be catastrophic!

Rudolph Steiner started from a similar insight. He believed that schools must meet students where they are, in specific stages of emotional and intellectual development that correlate with certain capabilities and interests. Instead of pushing a child to exceed or defy the stage she's in, he advocated matching the curriculum to mesh with her capacities, to fully activate and leverage her natural inclination to absorb new information and talents in developmentally appropriate ways. Steiner knew that learning was both social and emotional.

In early twentieth-century Germany, where the highly disciplined educational culture discouraged individualism and rewarded conformity, Steiner proposed a new model for teaching children that used the arts and music, nature and dance, gardening and knitting to encourage the individual growth of each child both as a student and as a human being.

In the words of Darling-Hammond and her coauthors:

> "The Waldorf instructional approach differs substantively from many other approaches to schooling in the United States. One of the key ideas that most differentiates a Waldorf education from other models is its ultimate goal: whole-life preparation. In addition to providing students with specific knowledge and skills to prepare them for college and career, a Waldorf education seeks to prepare children for meaningful lives in the broadest sense. It seeks to prepare students for physically, socially, artistically, and cognitively meaningful engagement with the world. A second difference is the extent to which Steiner's theory of child development and goals for nurturing human development inform every aspect of how children experience school." [36]

---

[36] Ibid., p. 21

In practical terms, this means that effective Waldorf teachers need training in Steiner's model of child development, as well as encouragement to shed a lot of what they were taught before. Because instead of teaching to tests, or even to grade levels, Waldorf teachers focus on how each individual child is progressing, adapting lessons and curricula so that every student can learn—on his or her own timetable. Teachers also stay with the same student cohort for eight years. Instead of seeing themselves as simply an elementary school teacher or a social studies teacher, they become mentors and guides to the same children for nearly a decade.

A totally new model of schooling means that parents, too, must adjust their expectations—of their children and of themselves. Instead of worrying that Johnny can't read yet, they can celebrate his ability to recite a beautiful poem, understanding that a love of language is the best foundation for learning to read and that reading skills will follow when Johnny is ready. Instead of viewing parental involvement as someone else's job, they have to be open to contributing to their child's education with their own time and efforts.

Needless to say, if the school's administration and district officials aren't on board, the whole program will collapse. All stakeholders have to be aligned—and that's always the barrier to change.

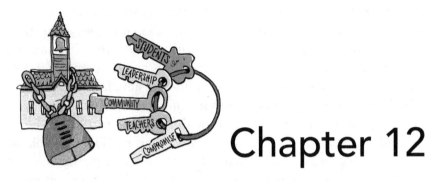

Chapter 12

Solutions: Five Keys to Reimagine Schools

Whether it's the Waldorf approach or another innovative model, changing the way we "do" school means overcoming the barriers of conflicting agendas and stakeholders. While every situation will present unique challenges and opportunities, there are five key components that must be addressed to succeed in an effort aimed at reimagining schools.

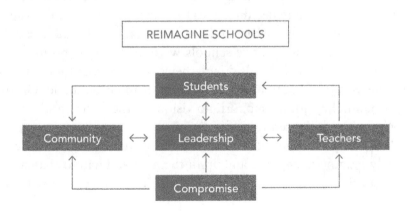

Key 1: Students

I've said throughout this journey that placing students at the center of the work of educating and developing children is always the place to start. It involves designing schools with their interests in mind and often involving them in the design process. When children can follow their natural interests, find excitement and passion, learning happens. This is what I refer to when I say learning is both social and emotional. What, where, when, and how do they want to learn? When we added a seventh Priority School, Rosa Parks Middle School, we specifically engaged groups of students in the reimagining process. When asked, students wanted more art, music, band, and dance opportunities in their new school. We listened. When the school opened to students in the fall of 2011, art, music, and band classes were there, too.

Key 2: Leadership

In my first one hundred days, as I went out into the district to talk to the community and visit schools, I realized that unlike Charlotte-Mecklenburg Schools—where we didn't have a wide variety of charter schools and other nontraditional models—part of the legacy of my predecessors (especially former Superintendent Rudy Crew) was a range of schools featuring innovative approaches such as the International Baccalaureate, College Pace, and Waldorf.

Yet there was a disconnect. The district central office had been operating the way many do: as a top-down, inside-out central command structure that issued directives from inside its four walls instead of getting out into the district and hearing what people had to say. As a result, the more innovative schools were in a strange position: As long as they kept their heads down, they could do what they wanted. No one was paying attention or holding them accountable. On the other hand, they got no support, no vision for the future, and no collaboration with the central office.

Some of these nontraditional programs were terrific, and my goal quickly became to energize and uplift them. First, I had to change the way teachers and principals viewed the central office, and with the help of some excellent colleagues, we went from an atmosphere of hostility and mistrust to mutual respect and open communication.

Some superintendents change central office culture by replacing much or all its staff, but I took a different approach. I brought in some trusted outsiders, but also sought out people already in the system who weren't being valued because they didn't fit the culture. By creating a culture of excellence and trust, we opened pathways for some really great district employees who rose to the challenge of a new way to lead.

I used to joke that as superintendent, I was in charge, but not in control. The truth is, every superintendent is in control of the vision for the district and the message we use to make that vision known. Once you establish and communicate that vision, you attract the people who believe in it and are willing to push it forward.

When it comes to models like Waldorf, the message should be carefully crafted. New programs take time to prove and the exercise of leadership includes persuading all stakeholders to have patience. That becomes very literal with Waldorf because students in earlier grades may be "behind" by traditional metrics, but then they leap ahead. That's how Waldorf works—it takes time to establish a love of language and learning, and then puts it in action.

The pace and timeline are different in the lower grades; you could even say they're slower. But the goal is for kids to develop a deeper level of understanding. Having teachers with the same class for eight years leads to efficiencies later, because the teachers and students know each other so well. The eventual outcomes are great, but any new model is going to diverge from established expectations. Leadership involves making the case for giving it time; otherwise, huge resistance will set in.

My outside-in approach also meant that we began by listening to the people in the district and finding out how to meet community needs. Alice Birney had a long waiting list, and that told us something right away. Families vote with their feet, and that parents were clamoring to get their kids into a Waldorf-inspired school signaled it deserved our strong support. Being supportive was not the same as letting the school run amok.

I had to make some tough calls about Alice Burney's curriculum. You'll notice in the chart above that leadership links directly to compromise. That's because in reimagining schools—as in other challenges an educator will face—modeling compromise is essential to getting everyone on the same page in terms of collaboration, respectful listening, and structural thinking.

When you look at any system as a whole—and in this case, that means a literal school system—you come to realize that it's not going to bend completely to your will. That's good, because no one is 100 percent right. Compromise is communication in action: listening to the needs and agendas of all stakeholders and finding a balance that moves your mission forward without leaving a trail of discontent, hostility, and resistance.

Offering support didn't mean that the folks at Alice Birney got everything they wanted. What it did mean was going to the union and negotiating for Waldorf-trained teachers. It also meant starting our own internal Waldorf credentialing program for teachers, who were spending their own money getting the training they needed—a real testament to their commitment.

I'll say more about the role of teachers further down, but I can't emphasize enough that in any reimagining process, teachers will make or break it. They are the ones on the front lines, and as they go through the day interacting with children, their attitudes will convey more to the community than any messaging campaign, newspaper article, or superintendent's speech. If you try to reach your objectives by threatening or bullying teachers, the community will eventually turn its back on you because children will be coming home unhappy and unable to learn.

To summarize the leadership traits needed for advancing a reimagining agenda:

- Promote and model healthy relationships: Change happens effectively in an atmosphere of trust. If you force change through with top-down directives, your outcomes will be unsustainable.

- Share your vision with a carefully crafted message: Change always takes time, and wherever there are competing agendas, impatience is the order of the day. Leadership involves persuasion, getting everyone on the same page, developing shared understanding, and setting expectations to give your program the time it needs to demonstrate success.

- Listen to the community: Students and parents will let you know what they want and need—if they feel safe talking to you and see that you're truly listening, not just going through the motions.

- Make the tough calls: Bringing leadership to a system that's been neglected is never easy. Some people won't get on board and will need to leave. Some programs won't operate the way they should and will need to be turned around or eliminated. You don't get to duck the responsibility of being the bearer of bad tidings from time to time.

- Model compromise: It's a major component to reimagining schools, and it has to start from the top.

- Give real support to teachers, who are central to any successful reimagining: Even if you have to get creative with funds or bend the rules, show the teachers you care and that you'll do what it takes to help them make the new program succeed.

- Celebrate what's right and the small successes: Doing so provides energy for the longer hauls.

Key 3: Community

"You want my son to knit? That's women's work!"[37]

A program like Waldorf is not going to appeal to everyone, especially if you don't go into the community and explain it. The first Waldorf-inspired school in Sacramento encountered so much backlash that it had to move to a different campus, leaving in its wake

---

[37] Ibid., p. 15

a lawsuit by a group of parents who had decided it was teaching "witchcraft" to their children.

The fact is, Waldorf is exceptionally effective at closing what people call the "achievement gap." Its supportive discipline practices, which rely on strong, trusting relationships between teachers and students, result in far lower suspension rates for all kids and close another important gap: the disproportionately high rate of suspension for African-American and Latino children. Compared to Alice Birney, the suspension rate for all children in SCUSD was eight times higher—and ten times higher for children of color.[38]

Children who get suspended tend to fail and drop out at higher rates, so this alone improves outcomes. But Alice Birney also succeeded in raising scores for all students in English language arts and mathematics. Notably, the improvements were greatest for traditionally underserved students, including socioeconomically disadvantaged students, African- American students, and Latino students.[39]

Unfortunately, some of the parents most resistant to the Waldorf approach came from these most vulnerable communities. It's understandable if you think about it. If you're farm laborer seeking a better life for your children, it would be disconcerting to find out they're spending classroom time planting and digging in a garden. That is, unless someone took the time to explain that planting and digging lead to an understanding of biology and prepare children to love science and have a bodily relationship to it. That way, they're more ready to one day become scientists and doctors.

Long after I left Sacramento, this contradiction continued to nag at me. Waldorf is incredibly effective at helping disadvantaged students succeed, yet today, as Darling-Hammond and her coauthors point out, "It tends to attract more educated, economically stable, and white families. Intentional efforts need to be made to ensure that such schools are both truly accessible to low-income families and families of color as well as are places where all families can feel a sense of belonging and value."[40]

---

[38] Ibid., p. 74

[39] Ibid., p. 76

[40] Ibid., p. 108

Those efforts at educating the whole community, I've come to realize, must be informed by the concept of equity. *Community engagement around reimagining schools must begin by a shared understanding of what equity means and how it is practiced.* People tend to confuse equity with the concept of "equal treatment," which means treating everyone the same. In fact, the two couldn't be more different.

It's easy to treat everybody equally. In the case of promoting a Waldorf-inspired school or another innovative program, you send out a flyer to every family in the district that explains how the program works and invite parents to an open house.

But what if some parents can't read? What if they speak only one of the forty languages used by the families in your district? What if the open house is scheduled in the evening, and some parents work nights? Equal treatment doesn't require empathy or compassion—all it takes is a Xerox machine, pumping out as many copies of the flyer as there are addresses on your mailing list.

Equity, on the other hand, requires a deep understanding of the community you hope to reach. It can mean unequal levels of effort aimed at the most disadvantaged, and that's okay. It's more than okay—it's equitable. Maybe reaching disadvantaged families means a home visit with an interpreter to explain how Waldorf lifts up children. Maybe it takes twice as long to persuade a farm laborer as it does a college professor, because the college professor wrote her master's thesis about Rudolph Steiner.

And believe me—you'll find pockets of resistance in every type of community. That college professor probably lives next door to a hyperaggressive, successful lawyer, and no son of his is going to sing madrigals and dance on a lawn!

Equity goes hand in hand with community outreach, if the outreach is going to succeed. That's why our district created Welcoming Schools and why we put so much effort into home visits. In an urban school district, you're serving families from all walks of life. Unless you think deeply about their differences and their varied needs, your plan for change is more likely to result in a lawsuit than a reimagined school.

Key 4: Teachers

I mentioned earlier that Alice Birney originated with a group of teachers who learned about Waldorf on their own and advocated for a campus to apply what they'd learned. This group, known as WISE (Waldorf Inspired Educators), got a head of steam under Superintendent Rudy Crew. However, with his departure, they found themselves in what one teacher called a no-man's land:

> "[T]here was no administrative support, we were all teaching at different schools, there was no core, and so we just kept meeting at different peoples' classrooms. . .we just decided we were not going to stop meeting. And so we kept meeting and we found a few little inroads, we found some special education money that we did some teacher training through that because, of course, movement and arts education and rhythm activities and all of those things that were good for special needs children. . . ." [41]

When they finally were assigned a campus, "the district did not approach the transformation of the school thoughtfully. They did not sufficiently address building teacher and community understanding or buy-in to the model. Rather, it was imposed on the community." [42] Without the needed leadership and community engagement, the school soon faced the lawsuit I referred to earlier, and was eventually moved to a new campus.

Those WISE teachers were assigned to the new school, and given the massive challenge of recruiting students to fill it:

> "[W]e literally went to door to door knocking on peoples' doors, like we looked for strollers in the front yard, they've got kids. . . . It wasn't a neighborhood school, it was just an empty building, and so we sort of canvassed the neighborhood and we got some people there." [43]

---

[41] Ibid., p. 14
[42] Ibid.
[43] Ibid., p. 15

Their trials and travails continued for some time before the program settled at Alice Birney and evolved into the success it is today. The details are less important than how Darling-Hammond sums it up: "Teacher involvement would be the core driver of the school as it matured. . . . [I]t was the teachers' clarity of vision that enabled the school to persist."[44]

You might notice that I haven't even mentioned the role of teachers in a Waldorf classroom, which, as I described earlier, is both far more demanding and far more rewarding than the traditional model. That's because before you think of them as teachers, I want you to see them as people, as dedicated professionals who were willing to do whatever it took to train themselves, advocate for their vision, and reach out to the community to fill their school and fulfill their mission.

In other words, these teachers were leaders. And in any community, you will find educators as inspired and committed as the WISE group. Here's the thing: Just like I found some of my best district staff hidden away in dusty corners because they didn't fit the central office culture, some of your best teachers may be far away from the spotlight in a badly managed district, waiting for leadership that recognizes and rewards passion and commitment, not following the rules and keeping your head down.

It's no secret that some people in the so-called "school reform" movement are at war with teachers' unions, and whether they intend it or not, are perceived as being at war with teachers themselves. What I learned in Sacramento, and keep learning as I move forward personally and professionally, is that no effort to transform a school or a district can succeed without *recognizing the dignity and worth of teachers* through appropriate compensation, opportunities for professional development, and positive, collaborative working conditions.

How much do positive relationships with teachers matter? I recently heard Professor Saul Rubenstein of Rutgers University describe his work with California's Labor Management Initiative, which promotes collaborative relationships between teachers' unions and public school administrators. You could easily anticipate that

---

[44] Ibid., p. 16

better communication and trust in this area would improve the experience of teachers, principals, and the staff at the central office.

But would you ever think a program that brings union leadership together with district leadership could improve student performance? That's what Professor Rubenstein is finding, and it doesn't surprise me. We saw this at our Priority Schools. Systems are just that: interconnected functions, all of which affect each other. Teachers touch and are touched by every aspect of a school system. Engage with them authentically and recognize their dignity and worth, and you're already starting to reimagine how schools work and how students learn.

Key 5: Compromise

In the chart above, compromise connects directly to leadership and affects the community and teachers. That's because everyone comes to the table with their own unique agenda, and every agenda runs up against the same obstacle: bureaucracies that operate on the school district, statewide, and national levels, and push back against change by their very nature.

On the district level, my team and I did what we could to shake loose money, find loopholes in the rules, and offer a compelling vision to support schools like Alice Birney, its community, and its teachers. We had a commitment, as Darling-Hammond and her coauthors put it, "to foster innovation and to allow some level of school-based decision making, [which] enabled Birney to maintain fidelity to the Waldorf approach."[45]

But if the school couldn't demonstrate success according to traditional metrics, our hands would be tied. However innovative, the school would rise or fall based on pre-established measures of student performance. That's where compromise was essential, and where leadership meant making tough decisions about what to hold tight and what to release. I felt comfortable giving Alice Birney, the Priority Schools, and other nontraditional schools a fair amount of freedom and flexibility in return for requiring them to meet fair performance targets.

---

[45] Ibid., p. 86

The school leaders had practiced compromise before. To meet the district's curriculum requirements, teachers had to harmonize Waldorf's unique approach with the standard, district-wide understanding of how a subject gets taught. All the teachers at the school worked together to synchronize district requirements with the Waldorf curriculum—and succeeded in satisfying the district that the Waldorf-inspired approach was legitimate and met its requirements.

In that case, compromise meant survival. In a system as complex as a school district, it often does—and it's important to communicate that survival may be at stake when you ask people to compromise instead of imposing requirements that, to them, seem unreasonable and arbitrary in a top-down manner. It takes vulnerability. Instead of being a general issuing orders to his troops, you're in the trenches, taking a risk by sitting down with people who may view you with suspicion and putting all your cards on the table.

When I arrived, there was a dispute over which mathematics curriculum Alice Birney would use. As much as I was committed to flexibility, in this instance I had to push back. The curriculum they wanted to keep, Saxon Math, had been proven less effective than the one chosen to replace it. So, given the need for our students to succeed—and for an innovative school like Alice Birney to offer objective data on its success—I advocated for the curriculum most likely to yield the best results. I also took the time to fully explain my reasons, answer questions, and offer context for my decision.

Over time, teachers and principals will see that compromising with the system isn't a zero-sum game. You may lose the argument, but win by serving your students the best way possible. That tension between district requirements and the unique approach of an innovative school encourages people on both sides to refresh their thinking. When Waldorf-trained teachers resisted standardized testing, for example, the principal at Alice Birney put a mirror up to their commitment to equity:

> "[The principal] talks with staff about how do we know if we're really meeting the needs of our English learners? How do we know if we're really meeting the needs of our African-American

students if we don't look somehow at test scores? There are some things that we can't just know from our gut and our heart, and they have because of that been much more open to that."[46]

It's a tightrope that must be walked with care. However, if you're upfront about your reasoning and demonstrate that you're willing to work to get the buy-in you need from the school and the community, resistance to meeting external standards will subside. What's essential is a culture of trust and mutual respect.

As shown in the chart, children, leadership, community, teachers, and the practice of compromise all operate in synch to produce an environment conducive to reimagining schools. If you expect to be heard, you must listen. You can't force change from unwilling people and expect a sustainable outcome. If you do it right, you contribute to the lifelong learning of everyone involved: students, parents, teachers, and — perhaps unexpectedly — yourself.

---

[46] Ibid., p. 87

Epilogue

"If you want to go fast, go alone. If you want to go far, go together." —African Proverb

Thank you for taking this journey with me, from the Commonwealth Corporation to Sacramento City Unified School District to the Stuart Foundation. From Mr. Boyadjian's geography classroom to the sparkle in Edwin's eyes when he knew an adult believed in him, and to Esteban E. Torres High School, where young people are at the center of their education. From the dawn of Whole Child education to the Alice Birney school. I hope I've helped you see public education through my eyes and, more importantly, through the eyes of the children it's meant to serve.

I hope you're inspired as I was by the young men who stormed the surf at the Naval Special Warfare Training Center near San Diego; that you are motivated by the students whose music education transforms their relationship to mathematics and learning; that you are moved by Anton and his classmates, who questioned school policy and challenged me to do something about it; and that you are appreciative of the gifted teachers, school leaders, and educators across the country who achieve great victories every day.

I hope if you're a parent, you'll join involved parents like Michele Brooks and countless others in pushing our political leaders, community and faith-based leaders, business leaders, elected school board members, and superintendents to step up to the challenge of meeting twenty-first-century educational needs with twenty-first-century solutions.

If you are an educator, I hope I have nurtured your belief in yourself, your enthusiasm for Whole Child education, and your commitment to the children you mentor and educate. If you are, or hope to be, a superintendent, I hope this book has helped you view your role in new ways, from the self-care you must practice, to the leadership your district needs from you, to the structural/systems approach you need to make lasting change happen.

If you are a policy maker, funder, or education advocate, I urge you to look at education with new eyes. Consider the history of our public education system and how it connects to the Whole Child movement. Consider how prophetic John Dewey's vision was, when he recognized that new technologies make it absurd to train children in rote tasks and narrow skills. Their future professions—especially in the twenty-first century —will require them to be intuitive, collaborative, compassionate, and self-aware critical thinkers.

I want to thank that mother who told me, "Superintendent, take risks for kids," and the students on those Green Teams who reminded me to use my extraordinary position to fight for all children. The light within children burns brightly if we look, believe, and stay patient. Imagine the possibilities if we think all children matter, if we believe in them, and if we hold them to the highest expectations?

Marc Johnson, former superintendent of Sanger Unified School District in California and a remarkable man and leader, once gave me a sunflower pin. He said he wore it to remind himself and others of all children and their potential. Sunflowers can stay dormant for years, and then—with the right amount of water, sunlight, and soil—they sprout and reach for the sky with all their brilliance.

"Children, are just like sunflowers," Marc reminded me. "We never know what might ignite their passions, interests, and learning, and therefore we can never, never, never, give up on a single one."

In this way, we are *all* called upon to be gardeners. Had all of us, as children, reaped the benefits of Whole Child education, we would hold this one truth in our hearts: In a society that's functioning at its best, there is no "your child" and "my child." These are all *our children*. For the sake of our collective future, I hope we realize this soon.

Acknowledgements

I tell people my career in education began in sixth grade. You'll have to the read the book to find out why. Along the way, I've been inspired by many extraordinary teachers, educators, and mentors—particularly those working in schools daily—some of whom are referenced here.

This book is written with immense gratitude to the Sacramento City School Board who hired and gave me an opportunity to help lead a very special school district. To my colleagues at the Sacramento City Unified School District with whom I spent four-and-a-half amazing years: Being your superintendent was the greatest job I'll ever have—and the hardest! I will never be able to adequately thank the thousands of dedicated staff, parents, and community members who worked—and continue to work—tirelessly for the children of Sacramento. Some staff, like Dr. Olivine Roberts, even moved to Sacramento to join our team and pursue this most noble work!

I am grateful to the Broad Academy and my advisers, mentors, coaches, and fellow superintendents, in particular Tim Quinn, Tom Payzant, Ray Cortines, Peter Gorman, Laura Schwalm and Dan Katzir.

To my first great teacher, Harry Boyadjian, who showed me the power of kindness, patience, and belief in others. His hand on my shoulder that fateful day, launched me on my journey.

I am indebted to Julie for following me first to Charlotte and later to Sacramento, enabling me to pursue my dream of becoming a school superintendent. Thank you for your love, support, and encouragement to pursue a career in public education. And to my children, Sylvie, Joey, and Gabi, and our dog Ruby, for your unconditional love.

Certainly, this book would not be possible without my parents, Sylvia and Bernard, who believed in the power of education, and who sacrificed so much to ensure my brothers, Michael and Bill, and I had access to the best.

To the unfailing support of the Stuart Foundation, and the guidance and expertise of Susanna Cooper, Koua Franz, Heather Randolph, and Maia Ettinger. To my friend and trusted advisor/editor, Mark McIntyre. You are the "Bill Russell" on my literary team.

And finally, to Jennifer Peck for her guidance, constant encouragement, challenging questions, support, and love.

Nothing we accomplish for children is possible without the above-mentioned support, encouragement, sacrifice, and love.

Thank you.

ABOUT THE AUTHOR

Jonathan P. Raymond is a passionate advocate for children with a long history of holding schools to higher standards, first as chief accountability officer of Charlotte-Mecklenburg Schools in North Carolina and later as superintendent of Sacramento City Unified School District (SCUSD). He led SCUSD, one of the country's largest, most impoverished and ethnically diverse districts, during the Great Recession. During his 2009–2013 tenure, he transformed some of the district's poorest-performing schools in the neediest neighborhoods to some of the highest performing, raised graduation rates, expanded early learning and summer learning programs, and introduced social and emotional learning to the curriculum. He is known as a bold leader who is determined and creative in his efforts to keep kids at the center within complex systems.

Raymond now serves as president of the Stuart Foundation, a California–based private foundation focused on systemic and sustained change within public education. Its guiding principle is an education system that values the Whole Child by strengthening the relationships between students, educators, families, and communities.

*In honor of my friends, coaches, and mentors
who have supported me on my journey.*

what
will you
feed

the flames
of passion?

what
will you
feed

the flames
of power?

what
truth will
you speak
to love

and how
will you
answer

the
call of
service

when
they know

your name?

—*Diane Cory*

CPSIA information can be obtained
at www.ICGtesting.com
Printed in the USA
FSHW01n0737120718
50355FS